ISRAEL AT FIFTY

Publisher: W. Quay Hays

Editorial Director: Peter L. Hoffman

Art Director: Susan Anson

Designer: Maritta Tapanainen

Production Director: Trudihope Schlomowitz

Color and Prepress Manager: Bill Castillo

Production Artists: Bill Neary, Regina Troyer

Production Assistants: Tom Archibeque, David Chadderdon,

Gus Dawson, Russel Lockwood, Roy Penn

Editorial Assistants: Dominic Friesen, Dana Stibor

Copyeditor: Karre Lynn

Photo Research and Selection: Dan Perry and Alfred Ironside

For information:

General Publishing Group, Inc.

2701 Ocean Park Boulevard, Suite 140

Santa Monica, CA 90405

Library of Congress Cataloging-in-Publication Data

Perry, Dan, 1963-

Israel at fifty / by Dan Perry and Alfred Ironside.

p.   cm.

ISBN 1-57544-079-2 (hc)

1. Israel—History.   2. Israel—History—Pictorial works.

I. Ironside, Alfred.   II. Title.

DS126.5.P47 1998

956.94—dc21   98-12589

                                                                          CIP

Printed by Worzalla in the USA

10 9 8 7 6 5 4 3 2 1

General Publishing Group

Los Angeles

ISRAEL AT FIFTY

BY DAN PERRY AND ALFRED IRONSIDE

Introduction by Shimon Peres

GENERAL PUBLISHING GROUP, INC.
Los Angeles

DEDICATION

*To our parents, Beatriz and Donald Ironside and Tilly and Mony Petreanu,
whose lives have inspired in their sons a deep appreciation of the past.*

ACKNOWLEDGMENTS

The authors would first and foremost like to thank the photographers, named and unnamed, whose beautiful and often courageous work brings history to life across these pages. We also extend our appreciation to the photo archivists and researchers at Israel's Government Press Office, the Associated Press, the Israeli newspaper *Ha'aretz*, the Foreign Ministry (whose web site was a terrific source of official historical texts), and the Israel Defense Forces, all of whom helped us in assembling the images. Our thanks go, in particular, to Itamar Grinberg and Hanan Isachar, who allowed us to spend hours culling their photos of contemporary Israel and whose work brings color and artfulness to the book.

We would also like to thank our many friends inside and outside of Israel who were a constant source of ideas and enthusiasm for our project. Our special gratitude goes to Dafna Linzer and Iris Perry, who were our first and best critics and our unswerving supporters throughout Israel's 49th and 50th years

TABLE OF CONTENTS

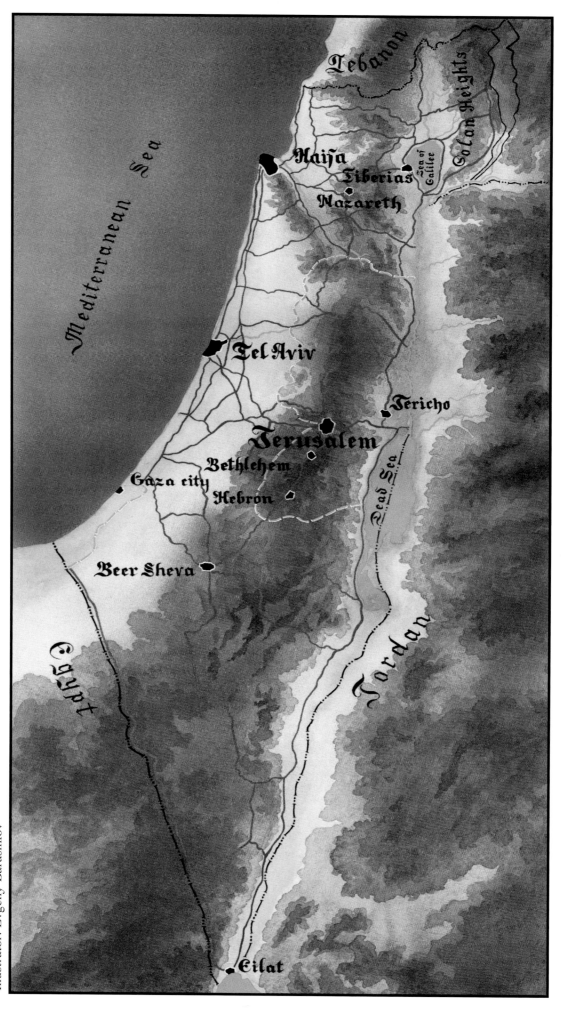

During its 50 years of existence, the attention of the world has been riveted on Israel, the focus of a remarkable 20th-century drama. The state was not born in a military crib, nor did it grow up in a political nursery. It was born as a dream and grew up as a prayer. It was a Utopian vision—maybe the only one to turn into reality this century. But even after the new reality became a fact, its actual existence did not cease to be questioned. The state was forced to go into battle five times, few against many; an embargo was imposed upon it by the Arab countries; the United Nations voted against it on a number of occasions; and to this very day, Israel has not been placed in any of the regional groupings of the United Nations.

And in spite of all this, Israel has not ceased to grow, develop, and uphold its democratic nature. First-class agriculture came forth from desert land; the Jewish people in exile gathered here from 80 countries around the world, practically performing an act of resurrection—reborn as an independent nation after a break of 2,000 years. Advanced technologies and modern industries were developed in this new country, an independent judicial system was created, as was an educational system of the highest order; and even while cannons thundered outside, heated debates continued inside the Knesset. Not a single day of war prevented one single day of democracy.

The powerful vitality these people displayed after being in exile for such an extended period of time, combined with the ordeal of an awful Holocaust, was extraordinary indeed. Despite differences on religion, despite Arab acts of terrorism, this nation set its sights on peace, even while in its midst a controversy on peace—and its price—is still raging.

Israel has proven that the strength of faith defies the power of statistics, and that the might of a people is not necessarily a mathematical equation, but a spiritual force.

The pictures in this album, like an echo in the mountains, do not tell the whole tale of Israel. But they do constitute the best testimony of its existence.

Shimon Peres

BUILDING A NATION

< Long before there was a state, the building blocks were laid >

ENVISIONING A NATION

In the midst of the 1897 Zionist Congress in Basel, Switzerland, Theodor Herzl stepped out onto a balcony and was captured in this famous moment of thought. "If you will it, it is no dream," Herzl wrote.

BUILDING A CITY

(opposite) In the first decades of construction, the Jewish founders of Tel Aviv had little more to work with than their own backs and those of camels. In 1936, members of the Zif-Zif gravel cooperative were moving sand and rock from the beach by camel caravan to concrete-manufacturing sites.

In 1909 they already had grand ideas. A local committee set out on foot from the port of Jaffa and walked north into the deep and mostly barren dunes along the sea. Standing above the Mediterranean on a cliff of sand, they could look inland as far as the eye could see. The view was almost unobstructed, and standing there north of ancient Jaffa, the fathers of what would become Tel Aviv took a moment to dream a city.

Then they began to build.

This book is about that process of building. It is a remembrance and a tribute to the people who came here—some before the state was officially founded, some after—and committed themselves to a role in the building of a shared home.

When you look around at Israel today it is hard to keep in mind that most of what is visible has been built in just this century, the majority of it in the last 50 years. It is easy to forget that while Israel was fighting five wars and an ongoing battle against terrorism and political and economic isolation, it was also building houses, draining swamps, and paving roads.

There was a remarkably efficient mobilization of people to patrol borders and fight wars—along with building a power station north of Tel Aviv, a port at Eilat, farming regions in the Negev desert, a phone system and a gas supply; and producing cars, clothes, refrigerators, schoolbooks, milk, and a political

TEL AVIV, 1910

Where a city now stands there were dunes. Setting out from the ancient port of Jaffa to claim the land to the north, Jewish pioneers surveyed a site for the first Jewish-built city in the modern world. They called it Tel Aviv—"Hill of Spring."

MEDITERRANEAN METROPOLIS

Tel Aviv in 1997. It is everything it would seem: a crowded place of business and beaches, falafel stands and high-rises. Seen as the center of Israeli hipness and pop culture, the city is also still home to many of the aging pioneers who built it.

AT THE BEACH, 1926

In its second decade Tel Aviv had acquired a scattering of buildings along its beachfront, where on weekends the town's residents valued their few moments of repose.

"Let the sovereignty be granted us over a portion of the globe large enough to satisfy the rightful requirements of a nation; the rest we shall manage for ourselves"

THEODOR HERZL,

DER JUDENSTAAT

(THE JEWISH STATE), 1896

system. It was done while absorbing wave after wave of new immigrants from vastly different backgrounds and cultures and teaching them Hebrew—a language that was only resurrected as a daily tongue in the 20th century specifically for this purpose.

Today, the raggedy façades of Tel Aviv, the city built upon the dunes, attest to more than just years of salt air and neglect. They tell of a city that in a few years went from several homes to hundreds, then to thousands, and is now the center of a vibrant metropolis of some 1.5 million people. They tell of a nation whose first concern was to get up and running, to get the basics in place. They tell of a place where things were built quickly so that the builders could move on to the next site.

The crowded, narrow streets that wind through the city's commercial districts, clogged with trucks and taxis and scooter delivery boys—where the front door was also often the loading dock—tell of the urgent need for commerce to unfold and grow. Likewise, that the city's first high-rise office building, the Shalom Tower, now stands completely isolated from what has become the central business district is not the embarrassment it would be in an American city; it is understood that the tower that went up quickly in the 1960s was a symbol of progress for a people for whom the symbol itself was important.

When Israelis stood on that dune and dreamed a city, they were actually dreaming a nation, and the spirit of building rolled on through the fields and bogs of the Galilee, under the twinkling stars of the Negev, beyond the alleys of Jerusalem, on the plains of the Jezreel Valley; wherever Jews had trickled in, wherever they were making homes, building a school, planting a garden, digging a drainage ditch, laying an electric line, establishing a synagogue. Long before there was a state, they built—out of conviction and belief that a new "Land of Israel" would arise, that more Jews would come, and that the world would acknowledge their right and their claim.

They built apartment houses, factories, and public edifices. They built a stock exchange. They devised a new irrigation system that used hosing with drip holes laid out along the rows of crops instead of sprinklers whose spray was partly lost. They slowly replaced smaller roads with larger highways, many leading to settlements in disputed territories.

While building up, they also dug down, exploring and excavating their own history and that of the many other civilizations that had lived in different periods on this land. They nonchalantly built around the crumbling skeletons of history, ultimately creating an identifiably Israeli juxtaposition of past and present. And they fashioned memorials and tributes to their mothers and fathers and those who came before them—and to those who were left behind.

AT THE OFFICE, 1998
The towers of Ramat Gan's business district along the Ayalon Expressway running through Tel Aviv are one of the country's main centers of business. They are also home to the country's diamond-polishing industry.

HEART OF A CITY

In 1934 (above) Dizengoff Circle was taking shape on the northern outskirts of the emerging city. Today the circle (at right), overlaid by an elevated pedestrian plaza with a fountain at its center, is surrounded by shops, movie theaters, and restaurants, including a McDonald's. There was a concerted effort to turn the sandy, barren town into a green, garden city—perhaps the most striking difference between the circle then and now.

A TOURIST MECCA ARISES

A view of Tel Aviv's central beachfront

in 1997. The towers at center are

nearly all hotels, capitalizing on the

city's beautiful setting facing the

western sunset over the

Mediterranean.

They also created institutions of learning and research and high-tech development that are producing breakthroughs across multiple fields. They built an army and the tools of war, and developed expertise in their application.

They forged a culture that borrowed many traditions from Europe, some from the Middle East, and new ones molded from the common experiences of privation, fear, victory, and remembrance. Slowly but surely they played a new music, wrote a new literature, and developed new kinds of humor and release.

And truly they created a distinct feel for their country. It has become a place with a character of its own that is part Brooklyn, part Krakow, part London, part Baghdad, part Miami, and a final part that is very strangely nowhere else, that is simply Israel.

On the ashes of the Nazi Holocaust, they tried their best to build a sense of security for the Jewish heart, a sense of belonging for the Jewish soul, a sense of vigor for the Jewish mind.

Israel today is an amalgamation of all that has been built so quickly, of all the vision and determination—and all the mistakes—of every soul that came to this place. That is why Israel is special—because one can still see the deliberateness and the human touch in everything that exists. Wherever one turns in Israel one can still detect the singular purpose that brought it into existence: the idea that the Jews had a right to a homeland in their historic birthplace.

> *"His Majesty's government views with favor the establishment in Palestine of a national home for the Jewish people, and will use their best endeavors to facilitate the achievement of this object."*
>
> **BALFOUR DECLARATION, WRITTEN BY BRITISH FOREIGN SECRETARY ALFRED J. BALFOUR TO JEWISH FINANCIER LORD ROTHSCHILD, 1917**

As the 1940s approached, and then unfolded in terror and calamity, Israel became no longer just an idea but a potential place of refuge. Through most of that horrendous time, the Jews were restricted by the British from immigrating to Palestine, but the movement already well underway served as a beacon of hope for a people caught in their loneliest and longest hour. There might be, after all, a place to go, where the community could join together and be rebuilt. Israel's existence became the ultimate expression of an irrepressible will to survive, not just on the part of individuals but for an entire people.

When Theodor Herzl envisioned a homeland for the Jews he was initially doubtful about how many of them would actually embrace the idea strongly enough to leave Europe. He selected Palestine, their historical place of origin,

OLD & NEW

When the city began, concrete was the material of choice and necessity. In many spots the fading and streaking façades of the early buildings stand in striking contrast to the steel and glass of modern construction.

LIVING IN LUXURY

(right) One of the first signs of prosperity was the elegant "City Garden" apartment tower and boutique shopping complex of the 1980s, built atop what was once the city's main zoo. Older residents of the area can easily remember the roar of lions at night.

as the best location because of his belief that it was the only place in the world with sufficient magnetism to stir the Jewish heart. Herzl, writing from the perspective of the late 19th century, envisioned an Israel as closely based on the European model as possible in order to attract the Jews of Europe, whom he saw as Israel's population, and to carry forward all the enlightenment and refinement that he felt Europe had attained.

Yet in a brutal irony of history the event that gave the final impetus to the foundation of Israel, the murder of six million Jews, simultaneously ripped from its infant grasp the people who were intended to be its population. For those who managed to get there, Israel was indeed a promised land, a place to replant the seeds of human dignity and a place to nurture them in the water of sweat and tears, work and remembrance.

Because it was a place born of such passions, and despite the unity and clarity the Jews brought to their lives in Israel, the country has also been a place of enormous conflict, a young nation without an exact set of blueprints for fulfilling that purpose.

For example, Israel's pre-state leader and first prime minister, David Ben-Gurion, had to reckon with the loss of most of Eastern Europe's Jews and find a way to sufficiently populate Israel so as to render it capable of defending itself. This was certainly a main reason for the urgency with which Israel invited the Jews of the Middle East to become part of the project—the first of many deviations from the essence of Herzl's vision. Other modifications would follow, including the formal creation of a role for religion in the state, the failure to write and pass a constitution, and the tolerance of an emerging class divide between the European Jews and the newcomers of Middle Eastern descent.

And tragically Israel has yet to realize Herzl's hope for harmonious, mutually beneficial coexistence with the Arabs. Virtually from the beginning there was bitterness and bloodshed.

As it turns 50 Israel has still not decided basic questions of nationhood.

This book will describe the moments of decision and indecision and their ramifications, as well as the moments of transcendent greatness, of national unity and celebration. The pictures and text that follow are intended as a tribute to a place born of extraordinary circumstances. They chronicle the building of a nation.

A MODERN PALACE

(left) The "Opera Tower" shopping and entertainment complex is one of the most popular gathering spots in Tel Aviv. In the 1990s dozens of American-style shopping malls sprouted—considerably altering shopping and leisure habits.

AN ANCIENT PORT RESTORED

(below) Biblical "Joppa" is mentioned in the Bible as the point of arrival for the lumber that built Jerusalem's temple, and the port from which Jonah sailed to his big fish. Since the 1970s Jaffa has been gradually restored to a glowing grandeur. The hill overlooking the ancient port has been transformed into an artist's quarter, and Arab fish restaurants and art galleries line its winding alleys.

CITY OF LIGHT

(right) The golden Dome of the Rock, which for many has come to symbolize the beauty and spirituality of Jerusalem, reflects, if anything, its legacy of conflict and conquest: The Muslim shrine was built atop the ruins of the first and second Jewish temples. Since the establishment of Israel, the Jews have enlarged the territory of their spiritual and political capital with acre upon acre of new construction, seeking to dwarf the Arab presence.

A HOUSE OF DEBATE

(above) Far from the parliamentary republic it would become, Herzl envisioned Israel as a democratic monarchy. He wrote that "a democracy without a sovereign's useful counterpoise...tends to idle in discussion in parliaments, and produces an objectionable class of men—professional politicians." In 1966, with great fanfare, Israel opened its new Knesset building.

THE NEW JERUSALEM

(below) Not far from the Knesset, the apartment towers of Rehavia strike a glamorous pose in the new parts of West Jerusalem.

As Israel approached its 50th year the last members of its founding generation—Yitzhak Rabin and Shimon Peres—were at the helm, with their perspective of the whole life of Israel guiding their decisions. Whatever the results of their actions, Rabin and Peres represented something Israel may have a hard time recapturing: the vision and moral authority of the founding fathers.

All over Israel, in places seen and unseen, from small kibbutz dwellings on the edge of a field to the most prestigious halls of the Knesset, the last of the founding generation is slipping away, men and women who survived the Holocaust, who were on board the *Exodus*, who fought in Israel's first war, who sacrificed so that their children could enjoy the Israel of today, and who protected those seeds of dignity when there was no sun and no water and no pure earth in sight. Quietly, in public ceremony and in private silence, they slip away, leaving behind a new generation of Israelis in a changed world.

Was the founding generation flawless? Undoubtedly not. Their time, the first 50 years of a new nation, was one of creation, of epic achievement, of declarations of freedom, of wars of independence, of stumbling experimentation and galvanizing purpose. Rife with missteps and loss, these years will nonetheless be remembered by the Israelis as a golden era of rebirth and purpose and youthful dreams.

The next 50 years may be no less critical than the first, and they will be judged more harshly. The time is at hand for introspection, for doubt, for improvement, for building anew, for doing better.

Israel at 50, a maturing nation, is fascinating for what it could yet be. The excitement of the project still tingles the spirit, the passion still courses through public debate, even as the vision has been supplanted by an increasingly sturdy reality.

The building of modern Israel may not be the ultimate definition of the Jews' place in the world, but one thing is sure: Something wondrous happened in the last 50 years, something worth noting, worth pausing to feel.

We are a people—one people.

We have honestly endeavored everywhere to merge ourselves in the social life of surrounding communities and preserve the faith of our fathers. We are not permitted to do so. In vain we are loyal patriots, our loyalty in some places running to extremes; in vain do we make the same sacrifices of life and property as our fellow citizens; in vain do we strive to increase the fame of our native land in science and art, or her wealth by trade and commerce. In countries where we have lived for centuries, we are still cried down as strangers....In the world as it is now, and for an indefinite period...I think we shall not be left in peace.

....No one can deny the gravity of the situation of the Jews. Wherever they live in perceptible numbers, they are more or less persecuted....

Attacks in parliaments, in assemblies, in the press, in the pulpit, in the street, on journeys...even in places of recreation, become daily more numerous....

The creation of a new state is neither ridiculous nor impossible. We have in our day witnessed the process in connection with nations which were not largely members of the middle class, but poorer, less educated, and consequently weaker than ourselves. The governments of all countries scourged by anti-Semitism will be keenly interested in assisting us to obtain the sovereignty we want....

We must not imagine the departure of the Jews to be a sudden one. It will be gradual, continuous, and will cover many decades. The poorest will go first to cultivate the soil. In accordance with a pre-conceived plan, they will construct roads, bridges, railways, and telegraph installations, regulate rivers, and build their own dwellings; their labor will create trade, trade will create markets, and markets will attract new settlers...

We could offer the present possessors of the land enormous advantages, assume part of the public debt, build new roads for traffic, which our presence in the country would render necessary, and do many other things. The creation of our state would be beneficial to adjacent countries because the cultivation of a strip of land increases the value of its surrounding districts in innumerable ways.

FROM *DER JUDENSTAAT* BY THEODOR HERZL, 1896

SYMBOL OF PROGRESS

(above) Much of the inland valleys of Israel's north were once so swampy that even water buffaloes roamed the area. To reclaim the land for agriculture, early settlers introduced the thirsty roots of the eucalyptus tree, now a common sight along the roads throughout the north.

TO GLOW LIKE THE SUN

(left) The moshav, a cousin of the kibbutz, was not nearly as ideological. Less interested in socialist ethos and absorbing immigrants, moshavs operated as straightforward agricultural cooperatives. Still, many moshavim took deep pride in their grand design, exhibited here by the sun's rays design of Moshav Nahalal. Today's moshavim remain a backbone of Israel's agricultural self-sufficiency.

POPULATING THE LAND

(above) Bet Hefer is one of hundreds of new towns and settlements built since the founding of the state. Sitting just inside the "green line" dividing pre-1967 Israel from the West Bank territory, Bet Hefer is still only 30 minutes from Tel Aviv.

POWERING A NATION

(left) The smokestacks of the Hadera power plant, halfway between Haifa and Tel Aviv, loom directly above the Roman ruins at Caesaria—an unintended but nonetheless instructive lesson in the comparative accomplishments of two civilizations.

SELF-SUFFICIENCY

In the early decades of the state agriculture was considered almost as critical to national survival as defense. The drive toward self-sufficiency succeeded in its primary goal but also made Israel a global center of agricultural research. However, the country is still better known for its oranges (above) than its wine-producing grapes.

NOT BAD FOR A KIBBUTZ

The idea of the communal farm struck deep roots in Israel. What eventually grew to be several hundred independent kibbutzim throughout the country were a pillar of Israel's economy and development. With the passing of the socialist era in the late 1970s, the kibbutzim were forced to change. Some are involved in industry, some have sold out to land speculation, and others have come to resemble affluent suburban enclaves, such as Kibbutz Dorot in the northern Negev Desert.

DESERT AS MOTIVATION

Far from deflating the early Israelis, the desert that occupies much of the country's south inspired ingenuity. David Ben-Gurion's vow to "make the desert bloom" is still pursued at the extensive research facilities of Ben-Gurion University of the Negev.

RED SEA RESORT

In one of the last stages of the War of Independence, Israeli troops pushed south to the Red Sea and planted their flag at an abandoned Egyptian outpost. Eilat, now an important port, giving Israel access to the Red Sea and Indian Ocean beyond, is best known as a getaway resort for Israelis and tourists from Europe. Beneath the sparkling surface of the Gulf waters lies one of the world's richest and most diverse coral reefs, attracting thousands of divers to its underwater treasures.

A TOUCH OF EUROPE

High above, on the 1,000-foot Mount Carmel, Haifa is a different world. Immigrants from Germany and other European countries established a sprawling, quiet, green settlement whose relaxed air remains far removed from the passions of the Middle East. Nonetheless, from the Haifa University tower at the crest of the mountain, a clear day can bring Syria into view.

A CITY OF INDUSTRY

Often compared to San Francisco for its natural bay and towering Mount Carmel, Haifa is, at its essence, a city of big industry, typified by the oil refineries to its north. According to local legend, when the city's first Jewish mayor was asked about Haifa's nightlife, he simply pointed toward the 24-hour factories glowing in the distance. "That's our nightlife," he said.

REMEMBERING THE HOLOCAUST

"Over 100 people were crammed into our railway car," the engraved text on the wall begins, and from the first few words the visitor is gripped. Israel's national Holocaust memorial, Yad Vashem, reminds its visitors that the Holocaust was not only a historical calamity that helped give rise to the state but also an ever-present impetus to live on, to excel.

גור, חסר האוויר. כל אחד מנסה להידחף

את אפי כדי לנשום מעט אוויר. הסרחון

כבת פתאום. לקרון נכנס אחד השומרים.

וא לקח כל מה שלא הוסתר היטב: כסף,

500 ו-1,000 זלוטי בעד מעט מים. שילמתי

ת התנפלה עלי אשה שילדה התעלף. בכל

ממנו. מרגע לרגע נעשה המצב בקרון קשה

תחתון. האנשים שכבו על הרצפה, נאנחו

חנה, רבים היו מוטלים על הרצפה, חלקם

חום ומחוסר אוויר..."

בקרון משא למחנה המוות - עדותו של ניצול

FUN IN THE SUN

On the beach in Tel Aviv young Israelis gather on summer evenings to watch the sun go down and party to the beat of bongos. Seventy years earlier their grandparents were still collecting sand to build the city.

FLOATING

A unique feature in the world, the
Dead Sea is a major tourist attraction
for visitors and Israelis alike, who
never cease to be amazed by their
buoyancy in the heavily salted water.

SKIING

To drive in a single afternoon from the Dead Sea, 1,312 feet below sea level, to Mount Hermon on the Golan Heights, at roughly 7,000 feet above, is one of the breathtaking experiences afforded by Israel's geographical diversity. The mountain also gives Israelis a much-needed escape from their desert surroundings.

A CAFÉ CULTURE

On Basel Street, a fairly typical city street in Tel Aviv, the corner café is the center of social life, equivalent to the corner pub in London. The shutters on the apartment houses are ubiquitous along the coast, an early reflection of the desire by European immigrants to reduce the dominance of the sun.

A PRE-STATE HEROINE

(above) In 1944 Hanna Szenes was one of 32 Palestine Jews who volunteered to parachute into Eastern Europe as spies for the British and organizers of Jewish resistance. A Hungarian native who had moved to Palestine in 1934, Szenes ultimately failed in her mission and was executed. But her bravery and daring became legend in Israel, and she was transformed into a national hero.

A BIBLICAL MATRIARCH

(right) The tomb of the biblical matriarch, Rachel, in 1933. Rachel's Tomb was a simple structure at the time of early Jewish immigration, visible along the road just outside Bethlehem. Today the site has become a virtual military compound: When Bethlehem became an autonomous Palestinian town in 1995, the tomb remained in Israeli hands, guarded by a phalanx of soldiers and barricades that dwarf the structure itself.

CHAPTER 1

REACHING FOR INDEPENDENCE

< Fifty years of determined struggle—and the Holocaust— give birth to modern Israel >

The story of the modern state of Israel does not begin in 1948. It really goes back another 51 years, to the last gasps of the 19th century, to the salons and libraries of old Vienna, where a young man named Theodor Herzl passed his days in heavy contemplation. There, snug within the cocoon of the Austrian Alps, Herzl surveyed the condition of The Jews and came to his fateful conclusion: the Jewish people needed a land of their own. They needed to return, he wrote, to "their ever-memorable historic home."

Born in Budapest, educated in Vienna, Herzl was a product of the diverse and cosmopolitan Austro-Hungarian Empire. Although trained as a lawyer he was a journalist by profession and, as a writer and later the literary editor for the *Neue Freie Presse*, he became interested in the situation of Europe's Jews. He initially believed that the Jewish people could survive and prosper in a multiethnic environment and, he hoped, assimilate into it. Gradually he changed his mind, concluding that for the Jews to be safe from racist oppression, their best option was to reunite in one place and establish a homeland.

In 1896, when Herzl published his ideas in *Der Judenstaat—The Jewish State*—the Jewish world had only recently emerged from centuries of relative isolation. The whole of the continent, in fact, was nearing the apex of an enormous era of change that had begun with the Renaissance in 14th-century

FORGING A STATE

Self-sufficiency was critical to the early Zionists. Long before the founding of the state, outfits like the Cluson steel foundry near Haifa Bay sprang up throughout the country.

POTASH WORKER

An early immigrant worker at a potash plant along the Dead Sea.

Italy, had continued through the Enlightenment of the 17th and 18th centuries, and was culminating in the industrial revolution of the 19th century. Throughout these centuries of change in Europe, religion had come under increasing intellectual assault. With the rise of mass communications—telegraph and telephone, with sound recording and moving pictures just around the corner— ideas were spreading like never before, altering not only the structures of governments and economies but also family life and the individual sense of destiny. In this world of change and ideas, as the Jews themselves were emerging from centuries of traditional community life, Herzl and others began to see how a national homeland for the Jewish people might not be such a wild dream.

But it was not just Jewish yearning or intellectual restlessness that gave birth to the idea of a modern Jewish state—it was practical conditions. In the late 19th century there were about 15 million Ashkenazi, or European Jews, and another 2 million who lived in smaller communities throughout North Africa and the Middle East.

Most of the world's Jews lived in parts of Eastern Europe and Russia, where life, in the midst of huge political and economic change, was becoming increasingly harsh for them. With the rule of the Russian czars collapsing, local chieftains were permitted to massacre and loot hundreds of the Jewish shtetls— the small rural communities that dotted the western frontier of the empire.

Elsewhere, in cities such as Minsk, Kishinev, Warsaw, Krakow, Odessa, Kiev, Chernowitz, and Bucharest, Jewish gains in mercantile trades, in education, in literature and art were often met with growing resentment by the local nationalities that in the past had often only sought to isolate and ignore the Jews.

But for Herzl nothing happening in Eastern Europe hit home with quite the same force as the Dreyfus Affair in 1894 France. Throughout Western Europe, Jews had been emancipated from political disenfranchisement in the mid- to late-1800s, becoming full citizens of the region's budding democracies, beginning to vote, growing part of the political and economic lives of their nations. Against this background the Dreyfus Affair—in which a Jewish French officer was wrongly accused and convicted of treason—was a huge shock to the Jews because it occurred in of all places Western Europe, which they considered so enlightened.

Herzl, who covered the trial as a journalist for a Vienna newspaper, began to see that, against their will, his people might never be accepted in Europe. He began his fight to galvanize Europe's Jews behind the idea of an independent homeland in Palestine, culminating in the 1897 Zionist Congress in Basel, Switzerland, which brought together hundreds of Jewish activists representing communities across the continent. Under Herzl's almost regal persona and leadership the congress decided to seek for the Jewish people "a publicly recognized, legally secured home in Palestine."

A SWAMPY SITUATION

In the first half of the century Israel's northern Hula Lake was home to a swampy mixture of reeds, mosquitoes, and water buffalo. As part of the effort to improve the land, the swamp was dried up in the 1920s and made into a cultivated valley and nature reserve. In more recent years environmentalists have condemned the swamp project as ecologically damaging.

BEACH FASHION, 1934

STRING SEXTET

You could take the Jews out of
Europe, but it wasn't so easy to take
Europe out of the Jews. This early
photo of classical music in the
wilderness illustrated one of the
striking paradoxes of Zionism.

ARAB RIOTS

(left) At the height of a wave of Arab riots, soldiers of the British Mandate repelled a stone-throwing horde from the Government House in Jaffa in 1937. Fifty years later the sight of Arabs hurling stones at soldiers would become a worldwide news story.

JEWS AND ARABS MEET

(above) In an effort to forge good relations, Jewish settlers from the Zichron Yaacov settlement near Haifa visit with their Arab neighbors. Many Zionists hoped that the Arabs of Palestine would welcome Jewish immigration as a harbinger of greater prosperity.

ive years later, at the age of 44, Herzl died. But the birth of a new nation had begun.

A growing stream of opinion held that Europe was not the place for the Jews. By 1910 they were fleeing war, dislocation, and discrimination in huge numbers. In those years more than a million went to America. A few tens of thousands chose Palestine, whose population was mostly Arab at the time.

They were not the first to arrive. In 1892 Jews constituted almost two-thirds of the 42,000 residents of Jerusalem, and were present in small clusters in Haifa, Jaffa, Safed, Hebron, and elsewhere throughout Palestine. Some were the straggling descendants of Jews who had never left. Others were there as the result of a steady trickle of immigration—not connected to the modern Zionist movement—that had gone on for centuries and had picked up in the 1800s. In the first decades of the 20th century these Jews were joined by Zionist pioneers who arrived in several waves—first from Poland

and Russia, then from Germany and Austria, soon even from Yemen.

Life in the early years was very hard. Water was at a premium in many parts of the country during much of the year; the soil was hard to bring to fertility; and a good part of the country was swampland where disease was spread by mosquitoes. And importantly, the small new settlements lacked the critical population mass necessary to make possible infrastructure projects and serious economic advances. Many of the newcomers scratched out a bare existence, and some died trying.

To help ease the way and establish beachheads for further immigration, a number of wealthy European Jews, most notably the Baron Edmond de Rothschild of Paris, became patrons of immigration, paying for the establishment of small settlements and outposts in Palestine. In places like Zichron Yaakov and Binyamina, on the coastal plains north of Caesaria, "sponsored" communities took root, but they struggled just the same.

Meanwhile, back in Europe, the Zionist

KIBBUTZ PROTECTION

Self-defense was essential to the early Jewish settlements in Palestine. Amid Arab rioting against the growing presence of the Jews in the 1930s, Jewish cavalry and foot patrols became a common part of pioneer life. The photo at left shows a unit of the JSP cavalry on patrol near Nahalal in February 1938. Above, a 1936 civilian guard escorts kibbutz workers through the fields.

cause was taken up by Chaim Weizmann, a Russian-born professor of chemistry. The soft-spoken but determined Weizmann moved to England in 1904 and began lobbying for British support. Eventually, in the midst of World War I, Britain was granted control over Palestine, as the crumbling Ottoman Empire finally receded after four centuries of rule.

Weizmann's greatest achievement came in November 1917, when Foreign Secretary Arthur Balfour sent Lord Rothschild a letter that seemed to commit Britain to the Zionist idea. It said: "His Majesty's Government views with favor the establishment in Palestine of a national home for the Jewish people, and will use its best endeavors to facilitate the achievement of this object." In a carefully worded reassurance to the Arab world, the "Balfour Declaration" also promised that "nothing shall be done that may prejudice the civil and religious rights of non-Jewish communities in Palestine."

Through the 1920s Jewish immigration continued to grow—to 400,000 by the late 1930s—most arriving through the port at Haifa, which had been rejuvenated by Britain and made the central portal into the region.

And something remarkable was happening once these "Old World" Jews arrived in Israel: They were transforming into a "new Jew"—the result of the early Zionist thinkers' strangely dualistic view of their own people.

On the one hand there was pride in their achievements; as Herzl put it in

WALLS AND TOWERS

The rough and isolated physical surroundings of many Jewish settlements suggest how determined the pioneers were. Much like the forts built to protect pioneers of the American West, Palestine's Jews built a series of "wall and tower" settlements to protect themselves from marauders.

Der Judenstaat, "our national character is too famous and, in spite of every
degradation, too fine to make its annihilation desirable."

But almost as powerful was a shame at the "abnormal" state of the
Jews as a people who were rootless. Their difficult history had made them
resourceful, but perhaps, it was felt, too meek, too compromising, even too
bookish, too inclined toward commerce and study. Better to turn them into
farmers and fighters, tanned and strong, depending more on their brawn and
a bit less on their wits. "Only when we will have learned the secret of labor
and committed to memory the hymn of those settled on their own soil shall we
deserve the title Man," wrote Yosef Haim Brenner, one of the most respected
Zionist ideologues of the early 20th century.

Many immigrants, whether they expected to like it or not, embraced
this idea and began to envision themselves anew. One of the most profound
manifestations of the drive to create a "new Jew" was the kibbutz movement.
Throughout the land self-styled pioneer farmers established agricultural
communities where the idea of voluntary communal living and egalitarianism
was paramount. The residents shared labor, social tasks, and even the raising of
children. The Hebrew word kibbutz literally means "a gathering together," and
thousands of new immigrants opted for this way of living, sharing what little
they had, tilling the land, and wearing cloth hats and sandals as the sun
scorched their skin. And they adopted a certain humility in the sense that
starting small and slowly building up was an honorable path.

There was another perhaps more remarkable part of the process: learning
Hebrew. Few Jews spoke Hebrew at the time that Zionism was created, and
practically none in everyday life. It was considered a holy tongue, relevant to
the study and ritual practice of Judaism but not at all appropriate for daily use.
Indeed, religious scholars and rabbis argued with conviction that the use of
God's language for any purpose other than worship would be blasphemous.
In any case Europe's Jews spoke other languages, of which Yiddish was the
primary common tongue. Its mixture of German grammar with Hebrew roots
was a peculiarly Jewish construct that also embraced Latin and Slavic
components where those language groups held sway.

Herzl thought the idea of renovating Hebrew impractical. Although he
hated Yiddish—which he derided as "these stunted, miserable jargons"—he
never came up with a solution to the question of the language of the Jewish
state. He simply decided that some language would prevail in the end.

A young man named Eliezer Ben-Yehuda saw it differently. If Herzl's
goal was the establishment of the state, Ben-Yehuda's was the establishment of
Hebrew as its official and natural language. Although he was reared in Lithuania,
Ben-Yehuda moved to Palestine in 1881 and militantly claimed Hebrew as his

one true language. He went through life building up its vocabulary, using roots from biblical texts to create new words for contemporary life.

His efforts to spread Hebrew among the people made him a rabble rouser in the eyes of Jerusalem's rabbis, and they conspired with the Ottomans, then on their last legs as rulers of Palestine, to excommunicate him from the Old City of Jerusalem and cause him other legal vexations. As a virtual one-man band, however, Ben-Yehuda never compromised, refusing to speak anything but Hebrew to his family and friends.

What ultimately kept his campaign alive were his newspapers. Subscribed to in the agricultural areas and kibbutzim that were so idealistically embracing the concept of the "new Jew," these outposts became the bedrock on which the seeping groundwaters of spoken Hebrew began flowing. And once the kibbutzim embraced the language, new immigrants would be exposed to it as they spent their first few years on the farms, helping cultivate the food and other basic products that were both their and the nation's sustenance.

When the Technion University in Haifa voted to accept both Hebrew and German as languages of scholarship in 1913, supporters of Hebrew launched a pressure campaign to eliminate German. The following year the university relented, and by 1916, 40 percent of the new settlement population was speaking Hebrew as a first language. Nothing would challenge it again.

For many of the early arrivals, adapting to the lifestyle of the new Jew was readily done. They were youthful, Zionist idealists seeking a fresh start. They

BARREN ROAD TO JERUSALEM
(below) An aerial view of Jerusalem's Old City in October 1937, and (above) a view of the barren hills to the east of the city along the road from Tel Aviv. These two photos illustrate how empty much of the now-disputed land surrounding Jerusalem was just 60 years ago.

DROP-OFF NEAR NETANYA

A Haganah vessel drops its illegal immigrant passengers into the shallows off the coast of Netanya in 1939. Tens of thousands of immigrants arrived this way after Britain announced its "White Paper" that year, restricting Jewish immigration. The restrictions, which helped Britain maintain some diplomatic leverage with the Arab world, were maintained through the war years and even during the postwar period.

had come voluntarily, out of a sense of adventure and a belief in the cause. But later waves of immigrants would be more rigid. The German immigrants of the 1930s were the first to openly cling to the mindset of middle-class bourgeoisie; rather than turning earth, they would own a shop; rather than eating around a communal table on a kibbutz, they would sit at a café in town and enjoy a good book. Later generations brought a variety of different attitudes, and political divisions among them would begin to emerge.

In the pre-state years the Arab population of Palestine would also grow. British rule brought relative prosperity and civil order to the region, reducing infant mortality and also attracting some people from neighboring areas. The Arab population in Palestine grew from 600,000 in 1920 to 840,000 in 1931.

Herzl foresaw good relations with the Arabs, and he set the tone for Zionist thinkers who assumed that the relative prosperity and advancement Jewish immigration would bring would win over the hearts and minds of the local Arabs. There even arose a Canaanite movement among the Jews, which saw the Palestinian Arabs as long-lost brothers and sought to encourage intermarriage and the creation of a new nation entirely different from the diaspora Jews, the term used to describe the loosely linked Jewish communities outside Israel.

The first Zionist to understand that such approaches would not work was also one of the most hard-line Jews: Vladimir (Zeev) Jabotinsky. The Odessa-born Jabotinsky organized a militia that fought alongside the British to remove the Turks from Palestine, then as a political leader demanded a firmer stand than Weizmann was taking for speedy Jewish independence.

Jabotinsky had no illusions about Arab acquiescence, a position that he presented as coming from respect for the Arabs' own dignity. In his book *A Hebrew State* he wrote of the Arabs: "The greatest folly would be to depend on the notion that our settlement will bring the natives much economic advantage. It is true—but no people ever sold out its national aspirations for a slice of bread and butter."

Jabotinsky led a breakaway faction called the Revisionist Movement, which disdained the pragmatism and willingness to compromise that typified the Zionist leadership. He held that the Jewish state should encompass territory on both banks of the Jordan River, including the part of British Palestine given to Transjordan after World War I. He predicted conflict and called for the creation of an army.

Indeed, the conflict soon began in 1921 with small-scale rioting. An intense wave of unrest came in 1929, as Jewish immigration continued rising. Arab riots erupted in Jerusalem and spread to other areas, including Haifa and Tel Aviv. In Hebron, the ancient Jewish community—then numbering about 60—was wiped out in a massacre. In almost a week of clashes throughout the territory, 133 Jews and 87 Arabs were killed. Such unrest continued in the

A STRIKING IRONY

In 1944, even as Jews in Europe were being herded onto death trains, immigrants at Haifa were transported in boxcars to reception camps in areas outside the city.

1930s, and Britain's inability to prevent or contain it deepened the Zionist ethos that the Jews must rely on themselves for their defense.

By the early 1930s the Jews had become well-organized around the Zionist cause. They had what amounted to an international legislature in the World Zionist Congress, which focused on setting policy direction and raising funds; a sort of administration in the Jewish Agency, which, although originally set up by the British, administered WZC decisions and oversaw immigration and construction projects in Palestine; and a national workers' movement in the Histadrut trade union.

There was a national leader in David Ben-Gurion, who was born in Poland in 1886 and immigrated to Palestine at 20; he became the leader of the WZC and was chairman of the Jewish Agency as well.

And there was an army of sorts: the Haganah, established in 1920, and its Palmach commando units. They were dedicated to protecting the lives and property of the Jews in Palestine and were tolerated by the British. But in 1931 a group of radicals formed a rival militia called the Irgun Zva'i Leumi (National Military Organization) and successfully sought Revisionist support. The Irgun adopted an activist policy opposed to the self-proclaimed "self-restraint" of the Haganah, which sought to avoid conflict with the British, and staged several attacks against British military posts, as well as Arabs. Its members were hunted by the British, in one period even with the active help of the Haganah.

In 1934 an 11-year-old boy from Poland named Shimon Persky set foot in Palestine. A few years later, as he stood on a highway outside Tel Aviv looking to hitch a ride, a car bearing Ben-Gurion pulled over. The fascinated youth, who later changed his name to Peres, became a protégé of the "Old Man," helping found kibbutzim, helping build Israel's air force and nuclear program, and as prime minister eventually becoming Israel's leading visionary of peace with the Arabs.

In the 1930s the urgency of getting Jews out of Europe was not yet clear, even to the Zionist leaders. Most Jews remained while Hitler came to power and began building his war machine. Large segments of the community could not quite believe that Hitler's rise could or would directly impact them. Even as Nazism grew and Germany tilted menacingly toward militarism and war, fewer than 100,000 Jews would make the deliberate decision to get out. For those who remained, bound together by daily ritual and the faith of generations, the impossible reality of their destiny would alight only gradually, first meeting disbelief, then terror, and finally a determined, proud effort to survive. For millions it would be too late; the full weight of human evil would ride them to their graves.

As war broke out in 1939—precisely the time Europe's Jews most needed a safe haven—Britain passed a "White Paper" severely restricting Jewish immigration into Palestine, a move aimed at placating the Arab powers in the region and improving Britain's positioning for a potential global conflict. It was, in essence, an abandonment of the commitment made by Britain in the Balfour Declaration.

Although the White Paper did not end immigration altogether, it provided for strict quotas that were hugely insufficient in the face of the threat to Jewish lives in Europe and the eventual tide of immigration it would create. In fact, the White Paper was a blueprint for crushing Zionism: Only 75,000 Jews would be permitted to arrive over five years, and then any further Jewish immigration would depend on Arab agreement.

Both the Haganah and the Irgun brought in thousands of illegal immigrants through the sea. Overcrowded fishing vessels, converted trawlers, and old ferries would sneak toward the coast of Israel, dropping their passengers into the coastal waters, sometimes several hundred yards offshore, forcing them to swim to safety. At times refugees were caught by British patrols and, in breathtaking episodes of the vagaries of war, taken to transit camps in Cyprus and elsewhere, where they would often be recycled back to mainland Europe.

Despite the Jewish outrage at the British position on immigration the Irgun ceased its anti-British policy and even encouraged its members to join the British army; Irgun leader David Raziel was killed in 1941 during a British raid in Iraq, and two years later Menachem Begin was appointed Irgun leader. Begin came to be regarded by the British as a terrorist, especially after the group blew up the British army headquarters at Jerusalem's King David Hotel in 1946.

When the guns fell silent in Europe, the world gradually awoke to the systematic slaughter of six million Jews by the Nazis. Only through the

BUCHENWALD SURVIVORS
Buchenwald survivors aboard the
Mataroa as it nears Halfa in 1945.

individual stories of survivors, the returning Russian, British, and American soldiers who had been their liberators, and the newspaper accounts of the slowly emerging evidence of atrocity did the world come to know of the extent and barbarism of the Holocaust.

Still, in the years immediately following the war Britain maintained its immigration quotas on Palestine, even as legions of Jewish refugees emerged from the rubble of central Europe desperately in search of a place for recovery, security, and renewal. Even as Jewish Agency emissaries traversed Europe extending a hand of hope and an invitation to Palestine to the shattered remnants of the continent's Jews, conflict between the British and the Haganah and the Irgun accelerated between 1945 and 1947, when Britain finally handed the Palestine problem over to the United Nations.

Acquiescence to the establishment of a Jewish state in Palestine was only a matter of time. Few countries outside the immediate region could bring themselves to publicly declare against the establishment of a Jewish state, despite the adamant resistance of the Arab world. The Holocaust simply left too powerful a sense of guilt in some, too compelling a cause of righteousness in others. The U.N. began work on a plan to partition the land.

For most of the Western world the 1940s are defined by the events of World War II. Even more than 50 years later, the dramatic moments of that time still capture this century's central contribution to the eternal drama of good versus evil and overwhelm most people's idea of the decade.

But for Israelis, perhaps for all Jews, the decade had a related but entirely different coda. For them the decade is heavy with the Holocaust but not overwhelmed by it—for in November 1947, and then in May 1948, there was something to celebrate. And in the year to follow there was a new war to fight— this time with the Jews armed and ready.

Patterns of Jewish settlement in the first half of the century made it such that when international mediators tried to devise a solution to dividing the land and setting up Israel, a natural, though imperfect, map emerged. The partition plan proposed by the United Nations in 1947 gave the Jewish state most of the Mediterranean coast and the Negev Desert in the south, and part of the Galilee in the north. It would have about 540,000 Jews and 400,000 Arabs—but its Jewish majority was expected to grow dramatically with the immigration of refugees. The Palestinian Arab state was given part of the Galilee, the Gaza Strip, and most of the hilly center of the country—the area now known as the

INDEPENDENCE

On the morning of May 14, 1948, the British lowered the Union Jack in Jerusalem. Fighting broke out across the nation by afternoon. At 4 P.M., David Ben-Gurion read the new state's independence proclamation at what was then the Tel Aviv Museum: "The state of Israel will be open to Jewish immigration and the ingathering of exiles. We extend the hand of peace and good neighborliness to all the states around us and to their peoples." Above, Ben-Gurion signs the independence proclamation.

EUPHORIA

Shortly after the declaration, several thousand people gathered outside the museum along Rothschild Boulevard to cheer independence. They jubilantly greeted the motorcade bearing members of the provisional parliament away from the venue.

West Bank. It would have about 800,000 Arabs and 10,000 Jews. Jerusalem, which had a substantial Jewish population, was to be an "international city" with no territorial link to the Jewish state.

On November 29, 1947, in a vote relayed by radio around the Middle East and throughout Palestine, the United Nations General Assembly approved the partition by a vote of 33 to 13, with 10 nations abstaining. For the Jews of Palestine it was a night of euphoria, a night in which the passing salutes of laughing strangers, the kisses stolen from unknown passersby, the revelry of running, walking, or driving through the streets proclaiming the news, can never be forgotten. It was the moment that millennia had reached for.

But everyone involved knew that the vote meant war. The Arabs of Palestine rejected partition, and there were justified fears that the Arab neighbors would invade as soon as the British departed. As they waited for the results of the vote the commander of the Haganah's Palmach commando unit had predicted to his men near Jerusalem that a war with the Arabs would cost the Jews 5,000 lives. His prediction would turn out to be just shy of the actual figure.

It took the British about six months to organize their full departure, and they did so after fighting had already broken out throughout Palestine.

Something unique occurred yesterday in Israel, and only future generations will be able to evaluate the full historical significance of the event. It is now up to all of us, acting out of a sense of Jewish fraternity, to devote every ounce of our strength to building and defending the State of Israel, which still faces a titanic political and military struggle.

Now is not the time for boasting. Whatever we have achieved is the result of the efforts of earlier generations no less than those of our own. It is also the result of an unwavering fidelity to our precious heritage, the heritage of a small nation that has suffered much, but at the same time has won for itself a special place in the history of mankind because of its spirit, faith, and vision....

But we should not deceive ourselves by thinking that formal diplomatic recognition will solve all our problems. We have a long thorny path ahead of us. The day after the State of Israel was established, Tel Aviv was bombed by Egyptian planes....We face a troubled and dangerous time...

It is the responsibility of each one of us, and of every municipal body, to take appropriate defensive measures, such as constructing air raid shelters, digging trenches, etc. We must concentrate in particular on building up a military striking force capable of repulsing and destroying enemy forces wherever they may be found.

Finally, we must prepare to receive our brethren from the far-flung corners of the Diaspora; from the camps of Cyprus, Germany, and Austria, as well as from all the other lands where the message of liberation has arrived. We will receive them with open arms and help them to strike roots here in the soil of the Homeland. The State of Israel calls on everyone to faithfully fulfill his duties in defense, construction, and immigrant absorption. Only in this way can we prove ourselves worthy of the hour.

SPEECH BY DAVID BEN-GURION, BROADCAST TO THE NATION ON MAY 15, 1948

SAMSON'S FOXES

A jeep from the Samson's Foxes unit on patrol during the War of Independence.

DAYAN IN HILLS

(below) Lt. Col. Moshe Dayan in the hills outside Jerusalem, November 1949.

On May 14, 1948, three weeks after the Jews took over Haifa and a few days after the British high commissioner had departed, Ben-Gurion gathered the leaders of the Zionist movement in a small auditorium on Rothschild Boulevard in what is now south Tel Aviv and, in a raspy, strident voice, began to read the Jewish state's declaration of independence. Golda Meir, the future prime minister, recalled sobbing as Ben-Gurion declared the country open to Jewish immigration.

The question of what to name the new nation was debated in the months following the partition vote. Some advocated Judah, others Samaria, the ancient names of regions surrounding Jerusalem, but in the end there really was little doubt. According to the Bible, the Jews became known as "the children of Israel" after God anointed Jacob, son of Isaac, grandson of Abraham, the patriarch of the Jewish people, giving him the name Israel. One of the ancient kingdoms established by the Jews in the region thousands of years later carried the name as well. Ben-Gurion announced the name of the country with characteristic drama and flourish.

"We announce thus," he declared. "The establishment of a Jewish state in the Land of Israel—the state of Israel."

Arab armies attacked Israel from the north, south, and east, and war raged for about a year. At independence, the Haganah counted some 10,000 infantry men, as well as aerial and naval companies, and it became the foundation of the Israel Defense Forces.

The Egyptian infantry invasion from the Sinai got to Ashdod, reaching what is now the "Ad Halom" (Up To Here) Bridge before being turned back and enabling the Israeli army to head all the way to the Red Sea. Egypt made do with the Gaza Strip, which was to have been part of the Arab state in Palestine. Syria's army didn't get very far. Israel took over that part of the Galilee that was to have been part of the Palestinian Arab state.

The most successful attacker was Transjordan—whose King Abdullah, ironically, was the friendliest Arab ruler. His Jordanian Legion seized most of the center of the territory allotted for the Palestinian state—the West Bank— and defeated Israel in several key battles, particularly in the Etzion bloc of settlements and the Latrun enclave. Transjordan also took over the eastern part of Jerusalem and the Old City, laying siege to the Jews who lived there and eventually forcing them out.

Israel's Harel Brigade, led by the young Yitzhak Rabin, blazed a path through the West Bank all the way to the western part of the city, which became part of Israel.

The War of Independence cost 6,000 Israeli lives—almost 1 percent of the Jewish population. But at the end, Israel controlled all the territory allotted the Jewish state in the U.N. plan and somewhat more, including half of Jerusalem. The Palestinian Arabs ended up with nothing; the war was for them an unmitigated political and personal disaster.

In the course of the war more than 600,000 Arabs fled the areas that came under Israel's control. Most of these people became refugees in Syria, Lebanon, Jordan, and Egypt. Even though only 156,000 Arabs remained as

FLAMES

Just after the founding of the new state, Begin's Irgun attempted to resupply itself with arms. Ben-Gurion warned that the new state could have only one military. When Begin tried to off-load arms from the Irgun vessel *Altalena* anyway, Ben-Gurion ordered it sunk. Several crew members were killed. The episode remains symbolic of the potentially explosive rift between the Israeli right and left.

DRUZE SOLDIERS

Although small in number, the Druze sect of Israel's Arab minority was loyal to the state from the beginning.

citizens of Israel at the end of the war in 1949, the community has since grown more than sixfold and now numbers one million, or about one-sixth of the current population.

This is potentially the key moral question of Israel's history. Some Israeli leaders, like Golda Meir, have claimed that Israel's leaders were saddened by their neighbors' flight and tried to discourage it. Whether or not this was true in some cases, there is no denying that tens of thousands were expelled from towns like Ramle and Lod, and "new historians"—particularly Benny Morris of Ben-Gurion University—claim that expulsion, or at least the threat of expulsion, was common.

In any case, Israel has refused to even entertain a return of the refugees, fearing that this would turn it into a binational state. The Arab states have done little to relieve the refugees' plight—using them, Israel argues, as a pawn to discredit the Zionist enterprise.

There is also debate today about whose was the stronger side in the war. For many years Israelis prided themselves on the inspiring victory of "few versus many." But the fact is that although the combined armies of Egypt, Syria, and Transjordan—which also received help from other Arab countries—numerically could have overwhelmed the Israeli army, the troops actually sent into battle did not; some of the Arab leaders, notably in Egypt, apparently feared for the stability of their regimes should troops be removed too far from the main cities. As the war dragged on Israel became better equipped than the Arabs, and there was no question that the Jews were the more motivated side.

Between February and July 1949, Egypt, Lebanon, Jordan, and Syria signed individual armistice agreements with Israel, negotiated mostly on the Greek island of Rhodes under the auspices of U.N. negotiator Ralph Bunche. The Arab states, grudgingly recognizing their defeat, signed the accords bitterly.

A new nation had been born.

Let us not be intoxicated with victory. To many people and not only among ourselves,

it would appear to be a miracle: a small nation of 700,000 persons (at the outset of the campaign there

were only 640,000) stood up against six nations numbering 30 million. However, none of us knows

whether the trial by bloodshed has yet ended. The enemy forces in the neighboring countries and in the

world at large have not yet despaired of their scheme to annihilate Israel in its own land or at least to

pare away its borders, and we do not yet know whether the recent war, which we fought in the Negev and

which ended in victory for the IDF, is the last battle or not, and as long as we cannot be confident that

we have won the last battle, let us not glory.

STATEMENT BY PRIME MINISTER DAVID BEN-GURION, JANUARY 12, 1949,

FIVE DAYS AFTER THE END OF THE WAR OF INDEPENDENCE

BLAZING THE TRAIL

(left) In the summer after independence, Israeli forces were deeply involved in the drive through enemy forces to open a channel to Jerusalem. Much of the fighting was done by the newly established Harel Brigade, commanded by the young Yitzhak Rabin. The narrow path they forged would remain Israel's sole link to the western half of the city after the war ended.

DAMAGED JERUSALEM

(above) The war took a toll on Jerusalem. Just outside the Old City, which the Jews did not succeed in capturing, the Notre Dame convent (in background) showed some of the heavy damage caused by building-to-building fighting.

THE ARMISTICE MAP

(above) Foreign Minister Moshe
Sharrett outlines the boundaries
agreed upon in the Israeli-Egypt
Armistice signed on February 24, 1949,
in Rhodes. Sharrett would become
Israel's second prime minister.

A FIRST BIRTHDAY

Israel celebrates its first
Independence Day in Tel Aviv with a
huge parade along Ben-Yehuda Street.

CROSSING THE DESERT

By September 1950 some 47,000 Yemenite Jews, the bulk of that country's Jewish population, had arrived in Israel. The establishment of Israel had made life in Yemen increasingly precarious. (above) Immigrants nearing the Hashed camp near Aden, 1949.

A NEW OUTLOOK

(opposite) A newly arrived Sephardi Jew contemplates life in the young state on a perch overlooking the isolated northern "development town" of Kiryat Shmona.

CHAPTER 2

THE INGATHERING

< The 1950s: some sailed, some flew, some walked across the desert; but they shared a common goal >

The founding generation of Israeli leaders were men and women of action, motivated by a deep belief in the justice of Zionism and galvanized by the Holocaust. With the War of Independence over and an armistice signed, Ben-Gurion and his colleagues quickly turned their attention to shoring up the foundations of the state.

The first priority was to fortify the nation's defenses. Not simply a matter of building tanks, planes, and munitions, it was, at its most fundamental level, a matter of populating the country. The borders needed to be defended, and the population had to be large enough to sustain a fighting force along almost 800 miles of shared border. By the end of the war almost 750,000 Jews lived in Palestine, most of them emigrants from Poland, Russia, and elsewhere in Europe. This was deemed insufficient to survive years of military struggle or develop an advanced economy.

The Zionist leaders had always counted on the eventual emigration of millions of Jews from Eastern Europe once the state was established. Now that community was decimated, and Ben-Gurion and his cabinet had to devise a new plan—the first major deviation from the Zionist vision set down by Herzl and pursued over the first half of the century.

They decided to send emissaries throughout the countries of North Africa and the Middle East to encourage and speed the immigration of the Sephardim—

> ### Every Jew has the right to emigrate to the country...
>
> *A Jew who comes to Israel, and after his arrival, expresses a desire to settle there may, while in Israel, obtain an immigrant certificate...*
>
> *Every Jew who migrated to the country before this law goes into effect, and every Jew who is born in the country, either before or after the law is effective, enjoys the same status as those who migrated to the country on the basis of this law.*
>
> **PART OF THE LAW OF RETURN, PASSED IN THE KNESSET ON JULY 5, 1950**

DIFFICULT EARLY DAYS

Many new immigrants were initially settled in this camp in central Israel, which grew into a town called Rosh Ha'ayin. The town remained almost exclusively Yemenite until the early 1990s, when its residents were joined by thousands of Russian immigrants.

MORE MOUTHS TO FEED

Children at the Beit Lid camp near

Netanya, January 1950.

Hebrew for "the Spaniards." These were considered the descendants and heirs of the great Jewish community that had lived in Spain until its expulsion in 1492 under the Inquisition. Some Sephardim had moved from Spain to Italy, Yugoslavia, Bulgaria, and Turkey, and became close to the broader community of European Jews that would, 400 years later, be represented at Herzl's congress in Basel.

But the majority found their way south out of Spain, crossing the sea to Morocco, Tunisia, Algeria, and Libya; some lived in more eastern territories that today are Syria, Iraq, Iran, and elsewhere in the Middle East. These Middle Eastern Jews—so different from the Ashkenazim (European Jews, from the medieval Hebrew Ashkenaz, or "Germany")—were really not a part of Herzl's plan.

Ben-Gurion's emissaries met Jews who had lived for centuries in Moslem societies of the Middle East and North Africa and who were relatively accepted and comfortable in their surroundings; certainly they never faced a total cataclysm of the kind the Ashkenazim did in Europe. Nonetheless, the creation

APARTMENTS IN THE DESERT

Beer Sheva, once an Arab trading outpost in the northern Negev Desert, was converted in the 1950s into a sprawling development town for immigrants from North Africa, Romania, and elsewhere.

of Israel had led to official hostility on the part of many Arab and Moslem nations, and Jewish communities throughout the region were ostracized, in some cases their very lives were in jeopardy. In Egypt, for example, Jewish activists were rounded up immediately following the creation of the Jewish state and tossed in jail. In other places the Jews were simply driven out, buffeted by a hatred whipped up by Arab politicians.

Thus, whether or not they had been happy where they were, many Sephardi Jews found they had little choice but to try to escape. And critically, among these highly traditional communities, even many who were not physically threatened felt the call of history—or God—and responded by moving to the new Israel.

From the southern reaches of the Saudi peninsula came nearly 50,000 Yemeni Jews, most in an airlift known as "Operation Magic Carpet." More than 120,000 Iraqi Jews arrived between 1950 and 1952. Some 300,000 Sephardim streamed in from Morocco, Tunisia, and Algeria, and some came from as far afield as India.

The mass arrival in Israel of these groups of Sephardi Jews, all significantly different in language and history from most of the veteran Israelis, would dramatically transform the character of a state founded on the aspirations and initiative of Europeans.

By the mid-1960s, the demographic balance within Israel had been overturned.

Many Ashkenazim watching the newcomers stream in shuddered at the sight of their brothers, whom they perceived as uncomfortably similar in appearance, behavior, and tongue to the Arabs, who were their enemies. A similar shock was often registered in the reverse: Many of the religious Yemeni Jews could hardly believe that the secular, sometimes atheistic, Europeans welcoming them to the Jewish state were Jews at all.

Nonetheless, to the Ashkenazi establishment, the immigration and integration of the Sephardim was an amazing success story. Jews from dozens of lands—radically different in every way—were transformed into a new society united in the purpose of survival. Hebrew became the lingua franca to them all. The army, into which nearly all Jewish men and most women were conscripted at age 18 for mandatory service of up to three years, was touted as a great equalizer, and in many ways was. In the army everyone wore the same pale green fatigues, endured the same rigors, slept in the same tents, and fought the same fights. More than anything the army—and Israel's state of siege—molded the immigrants into a new nation. The Sephardim became loyal citizens, the income gap between them and the generally better-educated Ashkenazim was controlled, and together they forged a democracy that, while imperfect and wobbly, was unlike anything seen in most of their native lands.

But many Sephardim remember only the humiliation of being sprayed with a DDT disinfectant upon arrival at processing centers.

They remember being consigned to distant outposts in the desert or in the hills, where there was free housing but often no work and generally little chance to advance. Most of all they remember the feeling that their Arabized, patriarchal cultural values were no good and that a new, quasi-European identity was being imposed on them by the school system, the media, the politicians, and their fellow Jews.

The fact is that the fledgling state was dominated by the Ashkenazi immigrants who had founded it. They were the bureaucrats who seemed to make every decision in every aspect of a socialist, statist society. When there were questions about housing preferences, the best jobs, infrastructure priorities, and so on, the system favored the European immigrant.

Probably the most striking outcome of this imbalance was in housing. In 1949, for example, when the cabinet debated whether it should favor a wave of emigrants from Poland in the distribution of new government housing, minister Yitzhak Rafael successfully argued that "if we release the Polish Jews from the (transit) camps and give them housing, they will get along easier than the Oriental (Sephardi) residents of the camps would, because they have among them professionals needed for the economy. This will be a blessing to the economy."

Furthermore, he said, "Polish Jews come from good living conditions. For them camp life will be more difficult than it would be for Yemeni Jews, for whom the camp is itself a salvation."

One of Ben-Gurion's important early decisions was to fortify the country's frontiers by populating not only the

interior of the country but the far-flung borders. So-called "development towns" were created as a matter of policy around the perimeter of the Gaza Strip, along the edge of the Negev Desert, and in otherwise less desirable stretches of real estate. Although there was never exactly a policy to populate these towns solely with Sephardi immigrants, that was largely the result.

In development towns like Afula and Beit Shean most Sephardim simply did not have the means to exploit the system the way the Ashkenazim were able to. An engineer from Romania who arrived in Israel in the 1950s was able to use his education and connections to find work in Tel Aviv and move there within a year or two. But it was likely that a merchant from Morocco and his family would remain in Beit Shean for generations.

Moreover, the government-created employment in development towns was mostly low-level industrial work. For many of the more educated Sephardim, and for the Sephardi elites who were successful in commerce in countries like Tunisia and Iraq, this was most deflating. Many Sephardim ended up trapped in development towns, unable to operate freely in a centrally controlled economy and with no one to champion their cause. For children and grandchildren of that era, the memory of a father or grandfather

THE TRIANGLE

Maj. Levinsky, the military governor of the Arab-populated area in central Israel known as "the Triangle," meets with village leaders in Taibe. Viewing this population as a potential threat, Israel imposed military rule on its Arab minority. In most cases, however, the Arabs lived peacefully, trying to make the best of their unique and problematic place at the fulcrum of the Arab-Israel conflict.

ICE PATROL

Ice for refrigeration was distributed by pull cart, with prices carefully controlled by the government bureaucracy. Here, a price patrol officer is on hand to prevent any ice-related infraction.

whose spirit was crushed by these circumstances would influence ethnic relations among Jews for decades to come.

For better or worse, the Ashkenazi establishment also moved to create a single Israeli "culture" based on European thinking and expression at the expense of the Arab influences more familiar to the Sephardim. The government controlled radio programming and Ashkenazim dominated publishing and filmmaking. In turn, these media promoted the idea of the new Jew and the new Israeli—icons originally created as a contrast to the "inadequate" European Jew but ones that still remained essentially European. Arab culture was marginalized and subtly delegitimized.

Many Israelis argue that keeping Israel "European" was essential to its ultimate success—that European culture was the foundation of Israel's solid educational system and judiciary, its ultimately stable democracy, and its powerful industry. But all of this had political ramifications that would come back to haunt the Labor Party, the successor of the determined establishment that ran Israel for its first three decades.

Meanwhile, severe austerity measures had been enacted after the War of Independence in order to allocate scarce resources to national priorities and build up key industries and civic projects. Israelis used coupons to buy rationed staples like gasoline, meat every few days, and flour. An entire generation of kids—Sephardi and Ashkenazi both—grew up on steamed vegetables and fried fish. There were just too many mouths to feed.

Ben-Gurion began to consider the unthinkable: reparations from Germany.

Only seven years after the Holocaust the idea of accepting reparations from the Germans was outrageous to many Jews, especially the hundreds of thousands of survivors living in Israel. Yet in Germany, postwar leader Konrad Adenauer used his character and integrity to forge a channel to Ben-Gurion (although the two would not meet for another decade). Adenauer was trying to help the healing of his own nation; Ben-Gurion was looking for resources to help grow his. It was a very difficult stand, yet Ben-Gurion made it, succeeding in getting Israel to begin forgiving West Germany by accepting financial reparations.

In January 1952 Menachem Begin, leader of the opposition Herut Party, assembled 15,000 people in the heart of Jerusalem and excoriated Ben-Gurion for accepting "blood money" from the Germans. His words were those of revolution: "This will be a war of life or death!" The crowd marched on the Knesset, where 500 police were waiting. They proved inadequate to contain the mob, and Ben-Gurion called in the army. Windows of the Knesset were smashed, and more than 100 police injured. After Begin suggested he might turn to physical violence against Knesset members to scuttle the reparations, the parliament withdrew his seat for 15 months. Ben-Gurion went on the radio and accused his rival of trying to destroy democracy in Israel. In the end Begin pulled back and the reparations were accepted, but the enmity between the premier and opposition leader was fierce. Ben-Gurion vowed that he would accept any party in his coalitions "except for Herut and the Communists."

But for Begin, being ostracized by the government would become the key to his later success. He would continue as an outsider, and he would attract in growing numbers the ranks of the overlooked and disaffected—the Sephardim, mostly—to his political coalition. He would, through the strength of his rebellious character, win their support for his right-wing, nationalist ideas, slowly building the party that would eventually topple the establishment.

But in the 1950s Israel was Ben-Gurion's country. In addition to austerity and reparations, the premier made several other decisions that would have lasting impact. One of them was his insistence on reclaiming parts of the Negev Desert for agricultural cultivation. He invested heavily in the southern town of Beer Sheva, "the gateway to the Negev," near where he built his personal home. "We will make the desert bloom!" he would say, and he fostered agriculture and irrigation enterprises devoted to doing just that.

In the years immediately after the War of Independence he also made fateful policy decisions regarding the role of religion in the state.

Many mainstream rabbis had initially been opposed to Zionism. A minority, led by Rabbi Avraham Yitzhak Hacohen Kook, felt Zionism might hasten the Jews' redemption. But, in the Hasidic and other ultra-Orthodox communities there was a strong feeling that, in the absence of an explicit order from God, establishing a Jewish state was sacrilege. Yet leading rabbis eventually emigrated to Israel to flee the Nazis. Even having done so, they would concede no more to what they felt was an unnatural condition of statehood preceding religion.

A FAMILY'S RATIONS

Mrs. Esar and her food rations: nine eggs (six for her son, three for herself); 400 grams of margarine; two tins of milk; three bags of sugar (1.5 kilos per person per month); and one bag of rice. She also got bread and white cheese, which were not rationed.

"Let not the murderers of our people also be their heirs!"

BEN-GURION, JANUARY 10, 1951, DEFENDING THE IDEA OF ACCEPTING MONIES FROM GERMANY

NO TO THE GERMANS

On February 5, 1952, young opposition firebrand Menachem Begin addressed thousands of Jews in downtown Jerusalem in a protest against David Ben-Gurion's decision to accept war reparations from West Germany. Begin took the issue to a nearly calamitous climax by leading a mob riot that damaged the Knesset building.

To win over the religious Ben-Gurion agreed to a series of concessions that were markedly at odds with the socialist, secular, and unified character he was trying to build in the state.

The rabbis of the "mainstream" religious movement—the *Mizrahi*, now known as the National Religious Movement—were given a host of powers relating to personal status issues: They would have dominion over marrying and divorcing Jews in Israel, burials, the granting of kosher food licenses, and so forth. Furthermore, the government allowed a second school system emphasizing religion to operate alongside the regular state schools.

For the tougher "ultra-Orthodox"—a community that maintained a highly religious way of life and kept the unique dress and traditions of their European forefathers—there were even more concessions. They were allowed to run an independent school system more or less as they pleased. Furthermore, the youth of the yeshivot—religious seminaries—were given draft exemptions. At the time these exemptions applied to only a few hundred, and they were seen as a fair means of rebuilding the world of Jewish scholarship that had been decimated by the Holocaust.

Ben-Gurion felt, ultimately, that religious Jewish opposition to the Jewish state was a bad thing. What would the world say about a Jewish state that was opposed by the most ardent upholders of Judaism?

Through the fifties the government also engaged in the creation of whole industries, setting up government businesses to power the growth of the nation. Israel Aircraft Industries was one of the first. The Dead Sea Works was expanded, and agricultural research, banking, and insurance institutions were supported and overseen. Many of the industrial enterprises were financed and run by American Jewish financiers such as Al Schwimmer, the founder of IAI.

The building of the state was as deliberate as possible in those years. Galvanized by the Holocaust and hastened by the ongoing threat from the Arab nations surrounding it, Israel—indeed, most Israelis—focused intently on national priorities and planned development and growth. It was a serious time, a time almost grave with purpose, a time when time could not be wasted.

MA'ALE AKRABIM AMBUSH
Attacks by fedayeen—guerrillas who infiltrated Israel's borders—caused hundreds of casualties throughout the 1950s and kept the Arab-Israeli conflict simmering despite the uneasy formal reprieve. Here, near the Ma'ale Akrabim outpost in the middle of the Negev in 1954, a bus ambush left its grim toll sprawled on the roadway.

The early 1950s were also a time of upheaval in the countries surrounding Israel, making the security issue all the more relevant. The Arabs had agreed to a cease-fire in 1949 but soon emerged as enduringly hostile to the Jewish state. Jordan's moderate King Abdullah was a potential friend, but he was assassinated by a Palestinian in East Jerusalem's Mosque of Omar in 1951. In Egypt a firebrand army officer named Gamal Abdel Nasser deposed King Farouk a year later. Nasser's driving ideology was Pan-Arab nationalism, and he cultivated warlike fulminations against Israel throughout the Arab world. Typical was Syrian President Shukri al-Quwatli's declaration in 1956: "The present situation requires the mobilization of all Arab strength to liquidate the state that has arisen in our region."

The Arab world was beginning to sense a new place for itself. With the passing of the Ottoman Empire, the departure of the colonial powers—France, Britain, and Italy—following the war and the rise of their modern states, Nasser's call for Pan-Arabism struck a chord of pride across North Africa and the Middle East. No longer would the Arab states be under the boot of outside empires. They would now take their rightful place upon the world stage and command the respect they deserved.

In this context the Arab leaders were stung by the emergence of Israel, which they saw as a European relic of the colonial era. And they were humiliated by the initial military victory over them. They found the Jewish interlopers a natural rallying point for their nationalist agendas.

There were constant incursions across the borders, especially from the Egyptian-controlled Gaza Strip, where tens of thousands of refugees from the nearby regions of Israel were packed into miserable refugee camps. Nasser allowed his territory to be used for infiltrations by fedayeen guerrillas who sowed death and destruction along the borders and in the heart of the country. Through the early 1950s hundreds of Israelis—most of them civilians—were wounded or killed in these attacks. Israel staged reprisals at least 14 times into Egyptian territory, other times into Jordanian territory. Sometimes Arab civilians were killed. The hatred on both sides of the border grew more intense.

In 1954 Nasser blockaded the Gulf of Aqaba, cutting off shipping from the south and effectively shutting down Israel's port at Eilat. A year and a half later, in July 1956, Nasser nationalized the Suez Canal, gravely insulting the British, who, according to a 1936 treaty, kept troops along the canal, and the French, who were dominant in building the canal and whose banking institutions still held its mortgage.

Unable to tolerate an indefinite closure on the Gulf of Aqaba, fed up with the fedayeen attacks, and threatened by the bluster of Arab leaders, Israel conspired with these two powers in launching an attack on Egypt in October 1956. Israel was to take the Sinai Peninsula and the British and French were to step in at the Suez Canal, commandeer it, and separate the Egyptian forces in the Sinai from reinforcements across the Suez.

On October 29 and 30, Israeli paratroopers seized the strategically crucial Mitla Pass in the northwest of the Sinai. Then columns of infantry and armor set out from the Negev toward Sharm el-Sheikh—freeing the straits of Tiran—through the center of the Sinai, and then into Gaza in the north. The French and British, in line with the secret planning of the operation, called on Israel to stop just short of the Suez Canal, and then invaded the canal zone themselves, ostensibly to secure it.

The operation was a military success but a diplomatic embarrassment. Combined U.S. and Soviet pressure in November compelled the French and British to withdraw from the canal region and forced Israel to hand back the Sinai. In exchange the United Nations placed a peacekeeping force along the Israeli-Egyptian border and, importantly, at the southern tip of the Sinai Peninsula to assure Israel of freedom of navigation through the Straits of Tiran at the mouth of the Gulf of Aqaba.

For Israeli moderates the Sinai campaign was the first in what would be a long series of frustrations. "The Sinai campaign was politically the most

unplanned war in history. We appeared before the whole world as tools of the imperialists," complained Israel's U.N. ambassador, Abba Eban.

A decade of sacrifice, hard decisions, and a second war was winding down. Israel could look back and feel that it had progressed greatly in the 1950s, but there was clearly still much to do.

One sign of that came in July 1959, in the ramshackle Haifa neighborhood of Wadi Salib, where a drunken Moroccan immigrant was shot while resisting arrest during a barroom brawl. False rumors quickly spread through the Sephardi community that he had been killed. A livid crowd gathered outside the local police station, and, after a period of building tension, police reinforcements from other districts stormed the crowd from the rear. Thirteen policemen and two civilians were injured and 32 protesters jailed in the resulting melee. The entire neighborhood was badly damaged.

It was a rude reminder that all was not well with the "ingathering of the exiles."

CHAPTER 3

COMING
OF AGE

*< The 1960s: The clothes in which the State
was founded no longer seemed to fit >*

THE DESERT COMES ALIVE

(above) "Making the desert bloom"
was a big slogan in Ben-Gurion's Israel,
but it was also a real challenge. One
of Israel's major achievements was
the invention of drip irrigation, where
water was distributed through fields
by means of rubber tubing.

**THE TOWER WITH
EVERYTHING**

(opposite) Israel's first modern high-
rise was the Shalom Tower in Tel Aviv.
Sitting at one end of Herzl Street, the
tower was a major symbol for Israelis
of their progress as a nation. It was
nearly 40 stories, rose more than 450
feet, and inside boasted elaborate tile
mosaics of events in Jewish history. It
also was home to the nation's first
department store, Kol-bo Shalom—
"Everything In It."

Although 1960 dawned much like 1959 and 1958 before it, the decade it announced was destined to become a watershed in Israeli history, altering its future course in dramatic ways.

As the '60s began Israel was still a humble nation with an inward focus. Its days as a flash point of international media attention were still invisible beyond the horizon, and though the country had been victorious in the Sinai Campaign, it had been a businesslike war that left few traces of pomp and circumstance. Much of the Western world was preoccupied with the Cold War, and the Middle East was still a sideshow, not a main stage like Southeast Asia or Cuba.

Alone on the periphery of the West, left to look after its own affairs, Israel was intent on consolidating its progress, building upon early foundations, and easing from a breathless sprint to a more steady marathon pace. The immigration wave began to die down. There were enough people to provide for a viable economy, a strong standing military, and a relatively vibrant society. It was time to build the ramparts of that society.

But first there was some unfinished business to attend to.

In its second decade, after tripling its population and building itself up, Israel was in a better position to confront its past. Throughout the early years of the state, the issue of the Holocaust had been surprisingly muted, almost as if it had been too horrific—or perhaps simply too recent—to address openly.

100 ISRAEL AT FIFTY

The Holocaust was a complex issue in Israel's developing national psyche. There was some suppressed guilt over the question of whether the people who lived there in the 1940s had done enough to help their brothers. There was some embarrassment over the notion that the European Jews had gone "like lambs to the slaughter," which at the same time fed the Zionist rejection of the "old" European Jew who had suffered oppression over the ages. And there was also a deep-seated fear that perhaps it could happen again, this time at the hands of the Arabs.

There were also those in Israel who were consumed by a lust for justice. It was known that some of the key architects of Hitler's Final Solution had escaped and were living secret lives in places like South America.

Hitler, of course, had committed suicide rather than face the world. His main lieutenants Hermann Göring and Joseph Goebbels were dead too, as was Reinhard Heydrich. That left Adolf Eichmann, who planned and oversaw the day-to-day operations of the death camps. He was found to be still alive and was viewed as a symbol of the many who had gotten away, and of the horrible injustice done to the Jews.

Isser Harel was a symbol as well—a symbol of the capacity the Jews had developed to right past wrongs. The shadowy figure was the head of the Mossad, which literally means the "institution"—Israel's version of the CIA. The organization had its roots in the illegal immigration efforts of the 1940s, and it helped arrange the quiet departure of Jews from unfriendly Arab countries in the 1950s. Gradually, it grew into Israel's main intelligence arm and would win worldwide acclaim through a series of spectacular successes, the first of which involved justice against the Nazis. Harel proposed a plan for the capture of Eichmann, which Ben-Gurion, in the strictest secrecy, approved. A team of agents was dispatched to Buenos Aires. For a period of weeks, they watched Eichmann coming and going from his home on Garibaldi Street, where he lived

> "I have to inform the Knesset that a short while ago the Israeli security services captured one of the greatest Nazi criminals, Adolf Eichmann."
>
> **DAVID BEN-GURION,**
>
> **MAY 23, 1960**

A GRAIN OF JUSTICE

In May 1960, Ben-Gurion electrified the Knesset with the sudden announcement that Adolf Eichmann (above), chief executor of Hitler's Final Solution, had been kidnapped in Argentina and brought to Israel. His trial, held in a Jerusalem auditorium, riveted the entire nation through the summer of hearings. The proceedings were somber, methodical, restrained, and often horrifying. Open to the public, thousands of Jews took part in personally witnessing Eichmann's prosecution (preceding page).

under an assumed name. When the moment to strike came, the Mossad kidnapped "Ricardo Clement," took him to a safe house for interrogation, then drugged him, put him on an Israeli plane, and secretly whisked him away.

On May 23, 1960, Ben-Gurion electrified the Knesset with the sudden announcement that Eichmann had been brought to Israel. A stunned silence filled the chamber, followed by a standing ovation.

Ben-Gurion was determined to avoid the appearance of a show trial. The government made sure that a highly solemn and official proceeding was arranged. Eichmann was allowed to pick his own counsel from anywhere in the world, and Israel would pay all legal fees and maintenance. Almost a year of preparation went into the trial, and when it opened in Jerusalem on April 11, 1961, an entire nation watched breathlessly. Hundreds of police were deployed to assure security for the proceedings, and Eichmann appeared in court—a converted auditorium—in a Plexiglas bulletproof box.

Israel's attorney general, Gideon Hausner, prosecuted. In his opening remarks to a packed gallery, he demonstratively asserted that he was not alone: "With me, in this place and at this hour, stand six million accusers."

The proceedings were open to public view and continued through the summer, each week offering new details of the Holocaust. Film reels of the atrocities, some made by the Germans themselves, were shown in open court as the gallery focused intently on Eichmann, their eyes glued to him in unspeakable incomprehension and anguish. On December 15, Eichmann was sentenced to death for 15 counts of crimes against the Jewish people: for "causing the killing of millions of Jews."

Eichmann's appeals to the Supreme Court and president of Israel, in which he argued that he abhorred the atrocities and had been just a "tool," were rejected.

He was hanged at midnight, on May 31, 1962. A police launch carried his ashes to the sea.

Ben-Gurion saw the trial as more than justice: It was an important event in the psyche of his country. He believed the efficiency of the Mossad and the thoroughness and fairness of the trial served to galvanize the Israeli character.

It was, in any case, a seminal moment. No one else has ever been executed in Israel.

> *"I had to obey the rules of war and my flag."*
>
> **EICHMANN**
>
> **BEFORE MAY 31, 1962**
>
> **EXECUTION**

Throughout the 1960s the government kept its eye on the strengthening of the Israeli economy and had developed the financial wherewithal to launch major new infrastructure projects. One of the biggest was the National Water Carrier. The carrier, completed in 1964, was a huge pipeline that drew water from the Sea of Galilee—Israel's only substantial source of drinking water—carried it to Israel's main cities on the coastal plain, and from there to the reaches of the desert in the Negev, which received three-quarters of its water from the pipe. It moved some 320 million cubic meters of water annually. There were also myriad other smaller water-conservation projects, ones that recycled sewage water, ran off rainwater, and harnessed small rivers to their fullest potential. In all, the water projects had massive implications for the economy as a whole, supplying the vital water that enabled industry and the population to grow at full force.

In this period Israel is also believed to have achieved the capacity to produce atomic weapons at the nuclear facility in Dimona, which was built in the late 1950s with the assistance of the French, then Israel's main ally. Although Israel has never admitted it has nuclear weapons, Dimona is widely reported to have yielded one of the world's most significant nuclear stockpiles, without a doubt providing a deterrent that amounts to one of the fundamental pillars of the country's defense.

Israel also drew the world's attention for its achievements in agriculture and de-desertification, pushing the Negev ever southward by using the locally invented method called drip irrigation, whereby a maze of rubber tubing is laid through fields, allowing a steady, controlled, direct-to-the-ground distribution of water with minimal waste and evaporation. Soon the country was dispatching technological-aid delegations to the rest of the developing world, from Africa to Southeast Asia. Potash and other minerals were mined from the Dead Sea area. A major administrative center was built in Beer Sheva, once a Bedouin trading post. A modern Mediterranean port was built at Ashdod, a fully planned city south of Tel Aviv.

Things seemed to be going quite well. Young adults who had arrived as immigrants in the 1950s were now having families. Parks and amusements for children started appearing. There was a special sense of romance and hopefulness in young couples and in the growing numbers of new parents as the first full generation of Israelis was born. In line with the continued feeling that people were needed—and with Jewish tradition—youth were encouraged to marry young and were taught that "children are a blessing."

MOVING WATER

The 1960s were a time of tremendous national economic growth spurred by government infrastructure projects. Perhaps the most celebrated of these was the construction of the National Water Carrier through the early- to mid-'60s, a project that brought freshwater from the Sea of Galilee to the center and south of the country.

As in the preceding decade, Israel was still tinkering with the creation of its unique culture, and the only network of radio stations was still run out of the prime minister's office. When the Beatles proposed a performance in Israel, there was official ambivalence to the idea of exposing the country's pioneering youth to such hedonism. In the end the concert was scuttled due to bureaucratic hassles involving the repatriation of concert proceeds.

Israel's own culture was in its infancy. The Middle Eastern part was still in a freeze, trying to find its bearings in a society established for Europeans. "Mainstream" culture had still not broken free of the rigid parameters imposed implicitly by a society under siege. Theater, comedy, and music troupes like Haim Topol's Batsal Yarok (Green Onion), and army troupes like the Nahal Brigade's band catered to an imagined yet rarely attained cultural consensus. Europeanized, motivated, socialistic, and puritanical themes were the order of the day in the unsteady but strangely content immigrant society. Popular music was still ideological and laden with simple nationalistic messages. Typical of the time was Shoshana Damari, a singer of Yemenite origins, whose romantic ballads were also very popular with Ashkenazim.

The consumer demands of the mass immigration, the rapid industrialization, and the prolonged relative calm on the borders created a period of sustained economic growth that by the middle of the decade landed Israel a decent place in the list of the world's relatively affluent nations (an achievement that must be viewed in the context of the fact that Western Europe was only starting to rebuild itself). Economic growth averaged almost seven percent a year in the first half of the decade. Foreign currency income from tourism reached the then-considerable sum of $56 million in 1966.

The Jewish state made another move that exhibited its gradual coming of age: It finally signaled some trust in its population of Arabs—the ones who had stayed after the state was founded.

In many cases the Arabs suffered land expropriations, mostly dating back to the War of Independence. Even many Arabs who remained in the country but had fled their homes were listed as "absentees." About 1,500 were expelled from "security zones" in various parts of the country. Only rarely were they allowed family reunions with the "Palestinian refugees" who may have been close relatives or neighbors a few years before and who now were living in other countries and had lost all claims on the land.

A STEP TOWARD PRAGMATISM

Israel's charismatic and visionary founder, David Ben-Gurion, resigned in 1963. His successor, Levi Eshkol, was more down-to-earth. Less concerned with the grand sweep of history, he focused on the practical needs of an emerging economy. He is remembered by Israelis for his steady hand in guiding the nation's development, as well as for his infamous stutters during a radio speech on the eve of the Six Day War.

Since the war the Arab communities had been under "Military Administration." This was applied in the northern Galilee region, where Nazareth and dozens of small hillside villages were located; in parts of the Negev, where a Bedouin population scratched a living from sheepherding and other small husbandry pursuits; an area known as the Triangle, north and inland from Tel Aviv, including small towns like Taibe; and Arab neighborhoods in towns like Ramle and Ashkelon.

The Arabs were citizens with the right to vote. But the Military Administration allowed the army to detain them without trial, to declare areas as closed military zones, to blockade neighborhoods, and to impose house arrests. It reflected Israel's suspicion that the Arab citizens were more loyal to their brethren who were refugees in neighboring countries than to their fellow citizens who were Jews. Many Israelis viewed the large and growing Arab minority—in a country under continual Arab threat—as a classic potential fifth column.

The Arabs felt like victims in this arrangement. In virtually all cases the Israeli Arabs were simply seeking a peaceful life. They had made their choice to stay when others fled, and they wanted to try to live a life on the land their families had, in many cases, dwelled upon for centuries.

It was becoming clear to the government that an internal understanding had to be reached.

Ben-Gurion, though, was not the man for this. He viewed the Military Administration as a necessary fact of life in an insecure region, and through two wars and constant security concerns as prime minister his position had embedded itself in his character. He finally resigned in 1963 over recriminations involving a spy scandal in Egypt known as the Lavon Affair, and was replaced by the more conciliatory Levi Eshkol, his onetime protégé. After three years at the helm, pursuing a steady-as-she-goes approach to steering the nation's growth and development, Eshkol decided Israel could afford to extend a hand to its Arab population. The military watch on the Arabs was lifted, and they became fuller citizens of the state.

CITIZEN ARABS

Prime Minister Levi Eshkol addresses a town meeting in Taibe in August 1965, where he received an enthusiastic reception. With Israel thriving, the prime minister would decide within several months to end the Military Administration over the country's Arab population and instate them as full citizens— a remarkable event for the Jewish state.

> *"The word has been given. Today we crush the hand that has reached out to strangle us....We did not want this war—the enemy did. And he shall have it."*
>
> **FLYER CIRCULATED TO IDF SOLDIERS ON JUNE 5, 1967**

By the mid-1960s the country's inward focus and strengthening were paralleled by a growth in external tensions with Israel's increasingly resentful neighbors, and the drums of war began beating more loudly once again.

In May 1967, Egypt's Nasser expelled the U.N. peacekeepers from Gaza and the southern tip of the Sinai, once again blockaded the Straits of Tiran to Israeli ships, and deployed his massive army along the Israeli border. To meet the threat, the much smaller Israel mobilized its reserves, a drastic measure which, had it lasted for a prolonged period, would have virtually destroyed the country's economy. Bus transportation was halted. Vehicles were commandeered for military uses. Men of military age were called to reserve army duty and replaced in their jobs by high school students. Normal life came to a near standstill.

Israel's situation was a strategic nightmare. At its narrowest point the country was a meager 12 miles wide. From the Golan Heights lurking just above Israel's northern border, Syrian soldiers overlooked Israel's best farmland and could, on a clear day, see across the Galilee to the Mediterranean. From the Gaza Strip the Egyptian army was within easy firing range of Israeli population centers. By the end of May Egypt had reached pacts with Jordan, Iraq, and other nations to fight Israel. It was a sign of the extreme feeling of emergency that the once-unthinkable Menachem Begin and his Herut Party were invited to join a "national unity government."

After three weeks of tension—known as the *hamtana* or "the waiting"—the Israeli military, led by Chief of Staff Yitzhak Rabin and newly appointed Defense Minister Moshe Dayan, received approval from Eshkol to launch a preemptive attack.

THE SIX DAY WAR

Two days following Israel's launch of the Six Day War, paratrooper commander Motta Gur (seated, on phone) looked out from Jerusalem's Mount of Olives and relayed the order for his men to begin their assault on the Old City on June 7, 1967.

Alone, unaided, neither seeking nor receiving help, our nation rose in self defense. So long as men cherish freedom, so long as small states strive for the dignity of existence, the exploits of Israel's armies will be told from generation to another with the deepest pride. The Soviet Union has described our resistance as aggression and sought to have it condemned. We reject this accusation with all our might. Here was armed force employed in a just and righteous cause, as righteous as the defenders of Valley Forge, as just as the expulsion of Hitler's bombers from the British skies, as noble as the protection of Stalingrad against the Nazi hordes, so was the defense of Israel's security and existence against those who sought our nation's destruction...

Never have freedom, honor, justice, national interest, and international morality been so righteously protected...

It may seem that Israel stands alone against numerous and powerful adversaries, but we have faith in the undying forces in our nation's history which have so often given the final victory to spirit over matter, to inner truth over mere quantity. We believe in the vigilance of history which has guarded our steps. The Guardian of Israel neither slumbers nor sleeps.

The Middle East, tired of wars, is ripe for a new emergence of human vitality.
Let the opportunity not fall again from our hands.

FOREIGN MINISTER ABBA EBAN AFTER THE SIX DAY WAR,

SPEAKING TO A SPECIAL ASSEMBLY OF THE UNITED NATIONS, JUNE 19, 1967

A SOLEMN PAUSE

(previous page) Humbled by history,
paratroopers pause before the
Western Wall, the last remnant of
the Jewish Temple destroyed by the
Romans nearly 2,000 years before.
Jerusalem's capture sent an electric
current through Jews all over the
world, both religious and secular,
and was seen by many as the final
capstone on a quest begun in the
1948 War of Independence.

A SPECIAL SOUND

(opposite) Military rabbi Shlomo
Goren, carrying Torah scrolls and
blowing the symbolic ram's horn,
brought a spiritual dimension to
the military victory.

Just before dawn Israeli warplanes headed southwest, following a course out over the Mediterranean toward 11 Egyptian air force bases. In a strike that lasted just less than three hours, 90 percent of Egypt's 340 combat planes were turned into smoldering wrecks, the majority of them on the ground.

No longer threatened from the skies, Israeli infantry and armor plowed into Arab territory, seizing strategic high ground and establishing, where possible, territorial buffers between the enemy armies and Israel's population centers. They captured the Golan Heights from Syria, the West Bank from Jordan, and the Gaza Strip and Sinai—again—from Egypt. In six days, Israel quadrupled its territory and utterly crushed Egyptian, Syrian, and Jordanian forces—as well as their pride.

For many Israelis the most gratifying moment came when paratroop forces led by Motta Gur ringed and took the Old City of Jerusalem. They gazed in wonder at the Wailing Wall—the last remnant of the ancient temple destroyed by the Romans some 1,900 years before—and at that moment and place seemed to represent millennia of Jewish longing. Soon military chaplain Shlomo Goren was blowing the ram's horn at the wall, and Dayan and Rabin marched into the walled Old City for a victory tour. For many Israelis only then was the War of Independence complete.

About 700 Israelis were killed in the six days of the war, but the Arabs claimed to have lost more than 10 times that. At the United Nations Security Council only four delegations supported a Soviet proposal to condemn Israel.

In the weeks and months that followed, Israel came to terms with what had transpired. In Jerusalem many Israelis returned to a place that they felt they had never left—even those who had never before stepped foot through its gates. Parents took children to see the captured tanks of Arab armies, which were put on display in town centers. Sons and brothers and fathers returned home to heroes welcomes. The army was the toast of the nation. The generals who ran the Six Day War—especially Dayan, with his famous eye patch—were treated like heroes who could do no wrong. The inaugural broadcast of Israel TV in 1968 was a military parade.

The war ended Israel's period of humility. It was not simply that it had been won: It had been won overpoweringly and swiftly. It had been won with an efficiency that few Israelis could have imagined. And it had come after a painful period of waiting and fear that had gripped the nation's consciousness like a vise.

Some felt the Six Day War was the cosmic inverse of the Jewish fate in World War II—that across the vast communal psyche of the Jewish people, reflected in all their individual actions and joint aspirations, there was a psychological gash, a sense of victimization or helplessness, fear or anger that was satisfied in some ineffable way by the war. The elation that erupted at the

end of that week was not just joy—it was a return to the sense that joy belonged in the world.

One of the spoils of war was the spurt of growth in the economy. Palestinian workers from the newly occupied territories were integrated into Israeli commerce, providing cheap labor and fueling a boom in productivity and profits. Israeli goods began creeping into the territories, just as a controlled flow of Palestinian workers began filtering into Israel proper to work day jobs before being escorted back to the border at night.

And of course, there was the land: Gaza, the Sinai, the West Bank territory itself, and the ancient heart of biblical Israel, the "Land of Canaan," the hills that were home to the storied crossroads of biblical history, including Jericho, Bethlehem, and Hebron. This was the land God had promised to Abraham, this was the land bequeathed to the children of Israel, and this was the land that Moses traversed in bringing his people home from bondage in Egypt. For Israel to control this land was exhilarating.

Indeed, the occupation of the Arab-populated territories completely shifted Israel's political course and injected new life into the Herut-Mapai divide. Suddenly Begin's theories about an expanded Israel no longer seemed utopian or out of touch. The new territories were there—they just needed to be controlled, annexed, populated. The question of whether to do this eventually overwhelmed everything else in Israeli politics, challenging Israel's democracy and its notion of what kind of country it wanted to be.

Israeli philosopher Yeshayahu Leibowitz was probably the first to identify the victory as a danger to Israeli society. He warned Israelis that there was no such thing as a "benign occupation" of a foreign people and that the norms of occupation could seep into Israel itself and undermine its tender democracy.

The Eshkol government at first seemed prepared to give up the territories. Only days after the end of the war, it offered the Arabs most of them back in exchange for peace. But the Arabs, shell-shocked and humiliated, did not respond. A few months later the offer was rescinded.

Some politicians began to view the West Bank and Gaza as an intrinsic part of Israel. Dayan said the West Bank was "the cradle of our nation's history...We have returned to Hebron, to Shechem (Nablus), to Bethlehem."

On April 4, 1968, less than a year after the Six Day War, a group of 10 Jewish families led by a rabbi named Moshe Levinger arrived in Hebron, a dense rubble pile of a town in the southern West Bank. The group pretended to

"If victory was not theirs, the alternative was annihilation."

MILITARY CHIEF YITZHAK RABIN AFTER THE SIX DAY WAR, EXPLAINING HIS SOLDIERS' MOTIVATION

War is intrinsically harsh and cruel, bloody and tear-stained, but particularly this war, which we have just undergone, brought forth rare and magnificent instances of heroism and courage, together with humane expressions of brotherhood, comradeship, and spiritual greatness.

Whoever has not seen a tank crew continue its attack with its commander killed and its vehicle badly damaged, whoever has not seen sappers endangering their lives to extricate wounded comrades from a mine field, whoever has not seen the anxiety and effort of the entire air force devoted to rescuing a pilot who has fallen in enemy territory, can not know the meaning of devotion between comrades in arms.

The entire nation was exalted and many wept upon hearing the news upon the capture of the Old City.... Nevertheless, we find more and more a strange phenomenon among our fighters. Their joy is incomplete, and more than a small proportion of sorrow and shock prevails in their festivities. And there are those who abstain from all celebration. The warriors on the front lines saw with their own eyes not only the glory of victory, but the price of victory. Their comrades who fell beside them bleeding. And I know that even the terrible price that even our enemies paid touched the hearts of many of our men...It may be that the Jewish people never learned and never accustomed itself to feel the triumph of conquest and victory and therefore we received it with mixed feelings...

All this springs from the soul and leads back to the spirit. Our warriors prevailed not by their weapons, but by the consciousness of a mission, by a consciousness of righteousness, by a deep love for their homeland, and an understanding of the difficult task laid before them; to ensure the existence of our people in its homeland, to protect, even at the price of their lives, the right of the nation of Israel to live in its own state free, independent, and peaceful.

This army, which I had the privilege of commanding through these battles, came from the people and returns to the people, to the people which rises in its hour of crisis and overcomes all enemies by virtue of its moral values, its spiritual readiness in the hour of need.

MILITARY CHIEF OF STAFF YITZHAK RABIN AFTER THE SIX DAY WAR,

IN HIS FIRST SPEECH AS A PUBLIC PERSONALITY, AT HEBREW UNIVERSITY, JUNE 28, 1967

VICTORIOUS GENERALS

With nearly 2,000 years of Jewish history and aspiration on their minds, Israel's victorious generals march into the Old City of Jerusalem after its capture on June 7, 1967. The Old City was finally back in the hands of a sovereign Jewish nation.

TAKING THE HIGH GROUND

On the fourth day of the war, Israel moved into the Golan Heights—the mountainous plateau on the border with Syria. Syria had used the Heights to shell Israeli villages in the valley below and to impede water flow into the fledgling state. On June 10, convoys crossed the Bnot Yaacov Bridge over the Jordan River, finding the surprised Syrians unready to wage significant battle.

be Swiss tourists and registered at the Park Hotel. The day after their arrival, Levinger announced that they were in fact Israeli citizens with intentions of staying and reestablishing the ancient Jewish presence in Hebron. The government at first opposed the move, then gradually relented, allowing the group to establish a settlement called Kiryat Arba nearby.

For many Israelis the question of the territories revolved around their strategic value. Others felt a deep historical resonance.

Levinger and his crowd felt something deeper still, something hard to argue against: God had given this land to the Jews. This idea would grow, gradually becoming the focal point of a poisonous political divide and dramatically altering the secular ethos on which Israel had been founded.

"We have returned…to the cradle of our nation's history…. We know that to give life to Jerusalem, we must station the soldiers and armor in the Shechem mountains and on the bridges over the Jordan River."

DEFENSE MINISTER

MOSHE DAYAN, AUGUST 3, 1967

"The Security Council (requests) withdrawal of Israel from territories occupied in the recent conflict."

U.N. SECURITY COUNCIL RESOLUTION 242, WHICH POINTEDLY OMITTED THE DEFINITE ARTICLE REGARDING THE LANDS ISRAEL SEIZED IN 1967

Following the war Israel began what would turn out to be an extended military occupation of more than one million Palestinians in the West Bank and Gaza Strip. Unlike the situation of the Arab citizens of Israel, the Palestinians of the territories remained politically disenfranchised and thoroughly under the boot of the Israeli army. (left) A group is rounded up in Hebron for interrogation by Israeli soldiers.

THE AFTERMATH

Hundreds of thousands of Palestinians in the occupied territories lived in refugee camps created after the Arab exodus from Israel during the 1948–49 war. The miserable living conditions in the camps sustained refugee bitterness toward Israel over many decades. (right) The refugee camp near Rafah, the southernmost town in the Gaza Strip, was particularly squalid.

GETTING MOD

(above) In the early 1970s Israeli culture expressed the new feeling that the sky was the limit in all areas of life. Fashion shows even arrived at military bases, where, in 1972, "the micromini with glass applications" was all the rage.

CHAPTER 4

ONTO THE WORLD STAGE

< The 1970s: From Munich to Entebbe to Camp David, Israel was everywhere >

Astrange item appeared in Israeli stores in 1970. The record named *Shablool* ("Snail") featured two bearded hippies on the cover. When a needle was set on the vinyl it produced the sound of a distinctly Western rhythm guitar with sexy lyrics about self-realization and having fun.

Arik Einstein and Shalom Hanoch were inventing Israeli rock, and it was more than music. It was the harbinger of a new era enabled by the Six Day War and by the psychological shift it brought to Israeli society. Nation-building as a personal project was beginning to fade among a new generation of Israelis. In its place came something unfamiliar: echoes of the 1960s counter-culture in the West. A homegrown "mod" generation arose. Cafés on Tel Aviv's Dizengoff Street overflowed with Israelis sporting long sideburns, bell-bottom jeans, and a fashionable nonchalance. New restaurants opened in rapid succession as Israel enjoyed a post-1967 economic and cultural boom.

Israel TV went on the air on Independence Day 1968, with the broadcast of a military parade. The one national network was all Israel would have for years, but even so, by the early 1970s almost every Jewish family had a TV in the living room—many of them large-screen cabinet-style sets manufactured in Germany. The TV age seemed to arrive in Israel at its natural moment: The nation that came of age in the 1960s was very eager, by the early 1970s, to admire itself in the pictures of the small screen, to see its progress glittering back. Television was a form of self-salute, both a product of the nation's industry and advancement and a medium for reveling in it—and ultimately escaping from it.

PART OF EUROPE

Mickey Berkowitz, captain of the
Maccabi Tel Aviv basketball team,
celebrating his team's entry into
the championship game of the
European Cup in 1977, which
they went on to win.

SPARTAN, IN A WAY

(above) Seventies-style consumerism represented the first major break with the spartan tradition of the socialist founders, who gazed in dismay at the parade of miniskirts, long sideburns, and bell-bottom jeans that became the symbols of Israel's emerging "me" generation.

The years of Israeli insularity were just about over, and the government's effort to shape the national culture would, with the introduction of TV, be forever affected. Israel's swelling pride was on grand, unconscious display almost nightly, and when the TVs went off in Tel Aviv and Haifa, people would stroll the major boulevards with a slightly different air than before, a new consciousness of seeing and being seen.

And as each viewer began to read their own meanings into the ever-changing images, so television began its inexorable process of altering the society and how its people saw themselves, their country, and their place in the world. More than anything, TV gave strength and ammunition to those individuals who felt suffocated by Israel's socialist, Zionist, statist environment. Emergent and rejectionist political and social movements finally had something to play off. Israel stood in front of the mirror for the first time and, without knowing it, began the long internal struggle of self-image.

As throughout Israel's history, the evolution of language reflected the greater evolutionary trends in society. Until this period the Hebrew propagated in public had been as stiff and formal as one would expect of a tongue that had to constantly be taught—not only to children but to the majority of the citizens who had to learn it as adults.

The early years of TV (and radio) reflected this well, with announcers forced to speak with "official" accents, stresses, and vocabulary markedly removed from the language as it was evolving on the street. In theater and at the movies an artificial-sounding Hebrew was the norm—as if the actors were using a lexicon borrowed from legal documents.

The rebellion against this most likely started with the most paradoxical of Israelis: Moise Tehillimzeiger, born in Poland in the 1920s. Upon arriving in Israel as a youth, Tehillimzeiger decided to not only become completely Israeli (before anyone knew exactly what this meant)—but to become the quintessential Israeli. He changed his Yiddish name to one more Hebrew— Dahn Ben-Amotz—and did everything to expunge every shred of Polishness from his character. In the late 1960s and early 1970s, Ben-Amotz seemed ubiquitous—mixing with all aspects of society and writing novels shocking for their grittiness and honesty. His key contribution to Israel's emerging culture, though, was probably the "dictionary" he cowrote documenting and inventing the "new" Hebrew, the real Hebrew, the Hebrew people actually spoke. It was a sensation, and it was important in dismantling the artifice of language in Israel by making clear that there was an alternative to the starched TV anchor. It would take about another two decades, but eventually formal Hebrew virtually disappeared from the airwaves too.

s Israelis' self-image developed so did their presence on the world stage. Prime Minister Golda Meir, an iconic Israeli figure who had nurtured the Zionist movement over coffee and cake in her kitchen in Jerusalem since long before the state was founded, was the guest of Richard Nixon at the White House. Golda, who was born in Russia, had immigrated with her family to the United States while still a girl, and grew up in Milwaukee. She married young and lived in Denver, where she found she was ill-suited to life as a housewife and was soon drawn to the Zionist movement and to life in Palestine. Now, 50 years later the mere sight of this diminutive old "Jewish mother," making quips in her well-preserved American accent that sent a charmed Nixon into uproarious laughter seemed to make Israel important overnight. And it reflected something more fundamental: The United States was becoming Israel's great guarantor, its ultimate ally.

In 1973 Israel was invited by Europe to participate in the Eurovision song festival, an international competition featuring middle-of-the-road songs

GOLDA GOES TO WASHINGTON

In the years that followed the Six Day War Israel stepped out onto the world stage in an unprecedented way. In September 1969, Golda Meir met with U.S. President Richard Nixon at the White House; the striking contrast in their personal styles was too visual for the media to resist. At a press conference at which she explained her opposition to a Palestinian state, Golda was asked for her gefilte fish recipe. "I'll do better than that," she replied. "When I come here again I promise to arrive three days in advance and make gefilte fish for lunch for all of you."

To me, being Jewish means and has always meant being proud to be part of a people that has maintained its distinct idea for more than 2,000 years with all the pain and torment that have been inflicted upon it....

We in Israel are only one part of the Jewish nation, and not even its largest part; but because Israel exists, Jewish history has been changed forever, and it is my deepest conviction that there are few Israelis today who do not understand and fully accept the responsibility that history has placed on their shoulders as Jews...

My vision of our future? A Jewish state in which masses of Jews will continue to settle and to build; an Israel bound in a collaborative effort with its neighbors on behalf of all the people of this region; an Israel that remains a flourishing democracy and a society resting firmly on social justice and equality...

I have seen my five grandchildren grow up as free Jews in a country that is their own. Let no one anywhere have any doubts about this: our children, and our children's children, will never settle for anything else.

GOLDA MEIR, FROM HER 1975 AUTOBIOGRAPHY, *MY LIFE* (DELL PUBLISHING, NEW YORK), JUST A YEAR AFTER BEING DEPOSED FROM THE OFFICE OF PRIME MINISTER IN THE WAKE OF THE YOM KIPPUR WAR

LET MY PEOPLE GO

Prime Minister Golda Meir leads a mass rally calling for the free emigration of Jews from the Soviet Union. The popular campaign was known for the slogan "Let my people go," and enjoyed moderate success, as from 1971 Moscow eased emigration policies for its Jews and tens of thousands got out.

catering to the broadest possible taste. A young singer known as Ilanit, whose
long blond locks and honey-sweet voice had made her the darling of the Israeli
pop scene, was dispatched to Luxembourg. When she won fourth place there
was a surge of national pride. Israel was part of Europe! A few years later there
was another ego boost when the Maccabi Tel Aviv team won the European
basketball championship; "We're on the map!" shouted the team's American-
born star Tal Brody.

The country's physical expansiveness, a consequence of the 1967 war, cured Israelis of the territorial claustrophobia many had felt before. They took road trips to Sharm-el-Sheikh on the southern tip of the Sinai Peninsula. They skied on the Golan's snowcapped Mount Hermon. They made excursions into the West Bank to see more of the Judean Hills.

The Palestinian Arabs of these territories, meanwhile, seemed to acquiesce to the new situation, with the exception of a few terrorist cells, which were put down ruthlessly. Israelis would justify the occupation with reassuring talk about how the "benign" Israeli hegemony was bringing the Arabs material and spiritual benefits that they would eventually learn to greatly appreciate.

But the opposite was true. The 1967 war had given rebirth to the Palestinians' national movement. When Egypt controlled Gaza and Jordan controlled the West Bank, there was very little talk of Palestinian independence. The "Arab state" that the U.N. had envisioned in part of Palestine was all but forgotten; there was only the Pan-Arab struggle against Israel in general.

Now with Israel in control of all the territory that had been earmarked for the Palestinian state, the Palestine Liberation Organization, set up in the early 1960s, had a clear role to play. The terrorist attacks launched to draw attention to the Palestinian cause were a brutal reminder that the conflict would not go away. One of the most devastating was the attack by the Black September group at the 1972 Olympic Games in Munich, when the world sat riveted to TV images of masked Palestinian gunmen moving about on the balconies of the Olympic Village, soon followed by the murder of 11 Israeli athletes.

Meanwhile, from Cairo came uncomfortable reminders that the conflict with the Arab states was far from over. Nasser's successor, Anwar Sadat, proclaimed he was willing to sacrifice one million men to regain the Sinai. But in Israel Moshe Dayan believed that "Sharm-el-Sheikh without peace is more important than peace without Sharm-el-Sheikh."

In the autumn of 1973 the CIA and Israel's Mossad provided intelligence information to the Meir government warning that Egypt and Syria were planning an attack. The information went unheeded. Meir and her cabinet could not imagine that just six years after the thorough beating that Israel had administered, the Arabs would try again.

It was a remarkable lapse.

Yom Kippur, the Day of Atonement—the holiest day in the Jewish

The 1973 Yom Kippur War caught Israel completely off guard. On October 6 on the Golan Heights, an Israeli force of some 180 tanks was overrun as it tried to hold out against a surprise Syrian armored assault.

calendar—fell on October 6. The streets of the country were empty and in its homes there was a murmuring quiet as the nation observed the traditional fast. Radio and TV were not broadcasting, virtually nothing was open, and no cars moved on the roads. On this day, with Israel at its lowest state of readiness, Egypt and Syria staged a mammoth surprise attack. The army was not prepared; many soldiers were on leave, and communications and logistics sites were staffed at a minimum.

Israelis turned on the TV sets to see Meir deliver a shocking message: "Citizens of Israel: Today at two in the afternoon the armies of Egypt and Syria launched an offensive against Israel. The Israel Defense Forces is fighting back and repelling the attack.... We have no doubt that the IDF will win, but we consider the resumption of the Egyptian-Syrian aggression as tantamount to an act of madness."

In the north, Syria began its attack with artillery bombardment and air strikes upon the sparsely defended Israeli positions, then swept across the

Golan with three Syrian infantry divisions and—at the height of battle—1,400 tanks to Israel's 180. They overran Israel's defenses and its positions on Mount Hermon, approaching the internationally recognized boundary

In the south some 70,000 Egyptian troops overran the 500 Israeli defenders holding the eastern bank of the Suez Canal. Their operation was carried out under the defense of dense antiaircraft fire, which effectively neutralized Israeli planes. The Egyptians established bridgeheads across the canal and began pushing into the Sinai with major tank power.

In Israel there was shock. At a news conference Dayan staggered military correspondents by suggesting he believed Israel might actually lose the war and be overrun. In public, however, leaders maintained bravado. "Our aim is to teach [the Arabs] a lesson and to win a decisive and significant victory—in short, to break their bones," said military chief David Elazar on the third day of the war.

TURNING THE TIDE

Israel launched a major counteroffensive and by October 10 had reclaimed most of its positions. Below, furious fighting raged on October 9, the same day that army Chief of Staff David Elazar arrived near the Golan front to oversee the counterattack.

A DARING MANEUVER

In the south, Egyptian amphibious units rolled across the Suez Canal under massive air cover provided by Sagger missiles launched from Egypt. Some 70,000 Egyptians were met on the Israeli side of the Suez by a force of fewer than 500 men. Israel struck back with a tank force stationed deeper in the Sinai. On October 15, a force led by General Ariel Sharon crossed the canal and managed to encircle some 20,000 Egyptian troops, a major Israeli maneuver that hastened the end of the war. Above, former military chief Haim Bar-Lev and Sharon (bandaged) review maps of the engagement.

"Our aim is to teach (the Arabs) a lesson and to win a decisive and significant victory— in short, to break their bones."

MILITARY CHIEF

DAVID ELAZAR,

OCTOBER 8, 1973

The United States and Soviet Union went on nuclear alert fearing that a desperate Israel would use its atomic bombs. To help Israel turn the tide of the war the United States staged a massive airlift of weapons and critically needed spare parts.

After 10 days Israel gained the upper hand and recouped most of its early losses before the fighting was halted under superpower pressure. In three weeks the country lost some 2,500 soldiers, a staggering number. Though it had emerged victorious, the nation was crushed.

An inquiry committee laid the blame for the debacle primarily at the feet of the military, but a public outcry against the government swelled and in April 1974 Golda Meir resigned. Yitzhak Rabin—the hero of '67—was given the reigns of the Labor Party and formed a new government.

The Mideast conflict quickly became a central problem for the world at large. First, the strategic importance of the region was reflected in the superpower nuclear alert during the war. In its aftermath, the Arab-led Organization of Petroleum Exporting Countries cut production, sending worldwide oil prices skyrocketing and causing major disruptions in the global economy, particularly in Europe and the United States. The oil crisis raised Israel's profile yet further as the United States began to see its strategic relationship with the Jewish state as one of increasing importance. That relationship would prove to be critical to Israel.

In Israel, the war was a political and psychological watershed. It emasculated the Labor Party leadership, first and foremost, for having left Israel so exposed and vulnerable. Israelis had hoped they were beyond such existential danger, and the comeuppance made them angry. The war destroyed the image of invincibility built up by the battlefield successes of 1948, 1956, and 1967. No less, it shattered the Labor Party's moral authority as the only force fit to govern. It opened the floodgates to all kinds of challenges to the justice and indomitability of the secular, socialist, Ashkenazi way of doing things that the Labor Party and its forerunner, Mapai, had always stood for. It brought to swift ripeness the rejectionist movements that Labor had successfully marginalized through a quarter century of rule. And ultimately it undermined the political and cultural monolith of Israel's ruling class through the rise of a Sephardi right-wing religious coalition.

Indeed, Israel had stopped building in the urgent and focused way it had in the 1950s and 1960s. After the Six Day War the nation went into a sort of cruise control, basking in its power and prosperity and growing culture until the Yom Kippur War gave a sharp new edge to the notion of atonement in 1973. Some of the more religious and traditional elements in society claimed they had seem it coming all along. Now that their point of view had been, in their minds, vindicated by the near disaster of the latest war it was time to push the attack forward.

Amid the tumult Rabin was received with great expectation. He was not tainted by the wayward years between the Six Day and Yom Kippur wars, having served much of that period in Washington as ambassador to the United States. He was also the first *sabra* prime minister—the first native-born Israeli to rise to the top job—and as such, in the eyes of many, was the embodiment of the country's coming of age. During his term, under the aegis of U.S. Secretary of State Henry Kissinger, Israel and Egypt signed a separation of forces agreement that went further than the deal made in the immediate aftermath of the war. It established a sliver of goodwill to the relationship of the two nations, as Israel returned to Egypt a significant part of the Sinai in the Suez Canal area, including the strategically important Mitla and Gidi passes.

Two years into his term, on July 4, 1976, Rabin was to oversee another great military operation: one small in scale but important nevertheless. On that day, Rabin dispatched airborne Israeli commandos some 4,000 kilometers

SELF-DEFENSE, SELF RELIANCE
Reflecting the state's relentless drive toward economic independence, government-owned Israel Aircraft Industries built and exported Kfir fighter jets in the 1970s. Israel's military-industrial complex also achieved world fame with the Uzi submachine gun and the Merkava tank.

A STUNNING RESCUE

On July 4, 1976, Israel welcomed home nearly 100 hostages rescued from terrorists at the airport in Entebbe. The Air France hijacking, which took the plane from Greece to Libya to Uganda, riveted much of the world, but, more importantly, the stunning Israeli commando raid on the tarmac at Entebbe greatly bolstered Israel's image as a special-operations juggernaut.

(2,500 miles) to Uganda for a mission that would forever imprint the name Entebbe into Israeli consciousness. A week earlier, Palestinian and German hijackers had commandeered an Air France jet and forced the pilot to fly to Libya, then to Uganda's Entebbe Airport, where they received the tacit backing of the country's leader Idi Amin, a former ally of Israel, who even boasted Israeli paratroop wings. The hijackers released most of the jet's passengers, holding only the crew and about 100 Israeli and Jewish passengers who had been on board. They demanded that Israel release scores of terrorists from jail. Israeli commandos took off in four transport aircraft from Sharm-el-Sheikh at the southern tip of the Sinai, the closest point under Israeli control, landing at the airport by night and taking the Ugandan defenders and the hijackers by surprise. Three Israelis were killed, including Lt. Col. Yonatan Netanyahu, one of the leaders of the operation.

The raid on Entebbe was hailed as a huge success, and the operation boosted Israel's image as a country emphatic in its refusal to give in to terrorism, and it helped restore some confidence in the military. It also deepened Israel's international image as something of a military and intelligence *wunderkind*.

But, in the end, the effects of the Yom Kippur War were much more powerful politically.

Until the mid-1970s, it was inconceivable for many Israelis to believe that the party of Ben-Gurion would not be in power, especially when the main opposition was a firebrand like Begin. But the mistakes that led to the war—the hubris, the blindness, the poor planning—were hard to forgive, even after Entebbe.

The Rabin government appeared to be paralyzed with indecision over what to do with the West Bank and Gaza. Labor's de facto policy had been formulated by former military hero Yigal Allon earlier in the decade. The plan called for the return of most of the West Bank to Jordan in exchange for peace, with Israel retaining some areas, including East Jerusalem and its environs and most of the Jordan River Valley, as a buffer against another armed incursion from the east. Consequently the Labor government annexed East Jerusalem and established some small desert settlements along the Jordan River. But Jordan's King Hussein was not receptive to the "Allon Plan," and the government did not seem to know where to go from there.

The opposition did. Begin and his party wanted the areas to be part of Israel. The West Bank was, in their eyes, the heart of biblical Israel, the cradle of Jewish civilization.

In the summer of 1975, a newly established group called Gush Emunim—"The Bloc of the Faithful"—set up an encampment on the ruins of ancient "Sebastia" near Nablus, the largest town in the West Bank territory. Rabin's government ordered the group to evacuate; they ignored him. Soon thousands

SUCCESS FOR THE SETTLERS
In 1975 Moshe Levinger (left)—considered the father of the West Bank settler movement—and young settler leader Hanan Porat were raised up by jubilant followers after the government hesitantly allowed them to maintain their encampment at Sebastia, in the northern West Bank.

Opposition leader Menachem Begin

toured Sebastia, lending legitimacy

to the efforts of the Gush Emunim.

of supporters joined their cause. For months the cabinet was undecided. By 1977, election year, Gush Emunim had established five settlements throughout the northern West Bank.

Spiritually Gush Emunim as a whole was an extension of the Levinger group that had settled near Hebron in the late 1960s, and it was an offshoot of the "national religious" movement, which had undergone a deep metamorphosis in the period after the Six Day War. In the past the National Religious Party had been moderate, and through its understanding with Ben-Gurion it was an automatic coalition ally of Labor Party governments. Through the years it espoused a nonaggressive policy, its leaders considering it unwise to tempt fate and anger the Arabs too much; in 1967—in a move that now seems incredible— it even counseled against taking the Old City of Jerusalem.

Now the national religious movement's agenda was gradually overtaken by Gush Emunim. A core group of ideologues in the movement began to see the issue of land as essential to Jewish redemption—a return to the land, control of the land, and sanctity of the land promised by God to the Jews. Anything else, in their minds, was secondary. Satisfying the national aspirations of the Palestinians was utterly absent from their agenda, and peace with the Arabs was not a priority.

Some of the members of Gush Emunim believed that a state of isolation and conflict might even be useful in ensuring the Jews remain a people who dwell apart, a people who do not assimilate into their region. To most Israelis Gush Emunim seemed to be nothing more than a nationalist group, and some even saw it as a modern embodiment of the pioneering spirit that typified the pre-state Labor movement. But in reality, it was a deeply devoted, well-thought-out religious movement that could pose a devastating challenge to the secular and moderate ethos Israel had stood for.

A few years later the extreme-right settlers would sprout a "Jewish Underground." Twenty-five men were arrested for a series of murders and crimes against Palestinians and spent several years in jail before being pardoned. The pardon itself was a striking illustration of the settlers' growing political clout.

The government's impotence versus Gush Emunim coincided with a growing awareness among the Sephardim of their political power. In the early 1970s protests erupted in low-income Sephardi neighborhoods in Jerusalem. This time the focus was on the absence of serious affirmative action for the Sephardim at a time when an early wave of newer emigrants from the Soviet Union were receiving tax breaks and mortgage advantages—the kind of financial aid no less needed by veteran Sephardi immigrants who comprised the bulk of Israel's poor.

The opposition Likud (Union)—a new bloc dominated by Begin's Herut—won support by attacking Labor as out of touch. Importantly, it proposed a series of free-market reforms that seemed to many of the underprivileged to hold out the possibility of breaking the Ashkenazi hold on wealth and advancement. Among much of the electorate, talk of a freer economy and greater individual opportunity struck a deep chord.

Labor won few friends with a series of minor corruption scandals by Rabin government officials, which nailed down the impression that the Labor Party had grown fat and stale and could do well with a period in opposition. The coup-de-grace came just before the 1977 elections when the newspaper *Ha'aretz* reported that Rabin's wife held an illegal bank account in the United States. Rabin resigned and was replaced by Shimon Peres, his defense minister and party rival, only weeks before the vote.

Labor was crushed, winning only 31 of the 120 seats in the Knesset. Likud won a stunning 47 seats and easily formed a governing majority with religious and other parties. For the first time, the party and people that founded the state were

"Between the sea and the Jordan, there will be Jewish sovereignty alone."

LIKUD PARTY

PLATFORM, 1977

MR. TELEVISION

One of the most familiar faces and voices in Israel was that of Haim Yavin (below), the man who sat at the anchor desk of Israel TV longer than any other. In 1977 Yavin spontaneously coined the word *Mahapah*—meaning "upheaval"—when announcing the election of the nation's first non-Labor government after nearly 30 years of statehood.

on the outside looking in and Begin, their age-old tormentor, was on the throne. Also for the first time the idea of a right and left in politics had practical meaning—Jerusalem was no longer a one-party town.

Those on the left had real fears about Begin. His past suggested he was an unpredictable and potentially violent leader who could lead Israel into a maelstrom. But he surprised everyone when, as a gesture to the old guard and a sign of his statesmanship, he invited Labor's Moshe Dayan to be his foreign minister. And a far bigger surprise was just around the corner.

In the years following the Yom Kippur War Egypt's Sadat had changed gears. Convinced that he could not win back the Sinai or bring prosperity to his country through war with Israel, he instead embarked upon a series of overtures toward reconciliation and peace.

Begin, in power for less than six months, responded by inviting Sadat to visit Jerusalem in October 1977.

Sadat wanted not only all of the Sinai back but a return by Israel of the other occupied territories to their previous owners. Begin wanted a territorial compromise in the Sinai. But after a year of fitful talks culminating in a marathon negotiation overseen by President Jimmy Carter at Camp David, Sadat and Begin struck a deal: Israel would return the entire Sinai—which Egypt agreed to demilitarize—in phases, dismantle its settlements, recognize "the inalienable rights of the Palestinian people," and agree to embark on negotiations, at first with Egypt, then perhaps with the Palestinians, over autonomy for the West Bank and Gaza.

In March 1979, the deal was sealed with a three-way handshake by Begin, Sadat, and Carter at the White House.

Within Israel the extreme right was outraged at the idea of returning territory, and the dismantling and bulldozing of the Sinai settlements, home to a few thousand Jews, was a dramatic and disturbing sight for much of Israel. Although Israel returned the Sinai, talks over the West Bank quickly bogged down.

Begin's ultimate objectives were not easily discerned. Even as he ceded the Sinai and engaged in talks over the other territories, he supported establishing footholds deep inside the West Bank, such as Alon Moreh near Nablus. His aim was to put as many Jewish dots on the map as he could. But knowing how few Israelis would make a dramatic move into the heart of the disputed territory, he also established settlements just over the so-called "Green Line," which marked the pre-1967 border between Israel and the West Bank territory belonging to

"In all sincerity I tell you that we welcome you among us with full security and safety...We used to reject you...We had our reasons and our fears, yes."

EGYPTIAN PRESIDENT

ANWAR SADAT TO THE KNESSET,

NOVEMBER 29, 1977

SHARED PAST, SHARED FUTURE

On one of several visits to Israel, Sadat was shown around Beer Sheva by Begin. The differences in their personal styles and political aims, compounded by each man's personal sense of pride, made for an uneasy rapport between them.

FEELING THE MOMENT

March 26, 1979: Sadat, Carter, and Begin in a memorable moment of spontaneous warmth after they signed the Israel-Egypt peace accord hammered out at Camp David.

Jordan. Settlements were built a few hundred to a few thousand yards inside the occupied territory, effectively "blurring" the border. Considerable tax advantages were offered to those who moved to the new locations, and slick advertising campaigns were launched, presenting settlements like Elkana as just another suburban development, "just five minutes from Kfar Sava," in Israel proper.

Beyond the commuter towns on the fringes of the border the interior of the territory was being dotted with small settlements as well. Over the next 20 years the numbers of settlers would steadily grow, eventually topping 150,000. It was as Begin believed it should be.

"We have a right and a demand for sovereignty over these areas of the Land of Israel. This is our land, and it belongs to the Jewish nation rightfully. We desire an agreement and peace."

PRIME MINISTER MENACHEM BEGIN'S PROPOSAL FOR PALESTINIAN AUTONOMY IN THE WEST BANK AND GAZA, DECEMBER 28, 1977

"*No more war, no more bloodshed.*"

PRIME MINISTER MENACHEM BEGIN, SIGNING PEACE TREATY WITH EGYPT IN 1979

VIEW OF THINGS TO COME

In the late 1970s and early 1980s
Israel increasingly embraced the idea
of settling the West Bank. Roads were
carved into the sides of barren Judean
hills; small, lonely outposts were
established in the Samarian highlands.

As the 1970s wound down Israel was a vastly transformed place. The war had halted the great trajectory of growth and development that had stretched from before the founding through the big 1967 victory. The Labor Party and its legendary leaders were outside government. Peace had been launched with Egypt, yet the country was distinctly unpeaceful in its body and soul. Terrorism struck repeatedly, and the PLO had made a name for itself with raids and attacks both within Israel and abroad. Israel was never again to be the small, isolated country that toiled in socialist purity toward a unified vision of the future.

Arik Einstein and Shalom Hanoch were still making beautiful music, leading an ever-growing community of Israeli artists forging an authentic and vibrant popular culture. But the leader of their band of bohemians was with them no more. Uri Zohar, the maverick comic genius who had directed a series of movies that glorified the hedonistic, womanizing, hard-drinking lifestyle in Tel Aviv, had repented completely, donning the black clothes and head gear of an ultra-Orthodox Jew in full view of a disbelieving TV audience before disappearing into a mysterious world of Torah study and constant worship.

A struggle for Israel's soul was beginning.

THE WEST BANK TRAIL

The settlers considered themselves important pioneers, but to others their move into the territory raised a frustrating barrier to an eventual settlement with the Palestinians.

CHAPTER 5

NECESSARY SACRIFICE

Despite his support for West Bank settlement, it was Begin who ceded the Sinai back to Egypt, resulting in the dismantling of several Jewish towns on the peninsula. For Israelis on all sides of the political spectrum, the sight of these communities being razed was discomforting and traumatic, a sensation exacerbated by emotional public demonstrations. Above, Yamit, the largest Sinai settlement, gives way to bulldozers.

NOW, THE TERRITORIES

The West Bank settler population exploded in the 1980s, growing from a few thousand to some 75,000 by the end of the decade. The Begin government threw considerable economic incentives at Israelis to encourage this growth.

(opposite) Begin and then-Housing Minister David Levy (in sunglasses) inspect progress on a settlement outside Jerusalem.

LOSS OF INNOCENCE

< The 1980s: For the first time,
the nation deeply questioned its fundamental
sense of righteousness >

The key events of the 1980s—the 1982 invasion of Lebanon to expel the PLO and the uprising that erupted in the West Bank and Gaza five years later—primarily concerned the Palestinians.

Begin continued building settlements through the early part of the decade, and their population—the "settlers"—grew to some 50,000 by 1989. Even for Israelis who did not approve of the construction, there was still a widely held belief that the military occupation of the West Bank and Gaza was "enlightened" and "benign." Relative to populations in the surrounding Arab states, the argument went, the Palestinians living under Israeli authority were better off than those living under Jordanian or Egyptian rule. And while some infrastructure advances were indeed made, there were practically no banks in the territories, Israel allowed little industry to develop, and there was often no electricity or water outside the cities. Hundreds of thousands depended on Israel for their livelihood, and although the salaries may have been good for the standards they once knew, they were learning to apply Israeli—or Western—standards, and knew they were being oppressed.

Already a generation had been born under a siege mentality, and many of them were thoroughly entrenched in a "refugee" way of life, never quite belonging anywhere, not part of any national home. It was through this more fundamental truth that the PLO continued to grow in its influence and support, particularly through activity in southern Lebanon, from which it was becoming proficient at staging incursions and launching missiles against Israel.

BEIRUT UNDER SIEGE

The 1982 invasion of Lebanon was supposed to last only a few weeks, but two months later Israeli forces had surged all the way to Beirut. The goal: to root out the PLO by siege and bombardment. Above, an Israeli Phantom jet soars over the Lebanese capital.

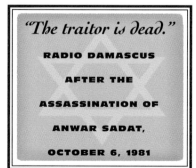

"The traitor is dead."

RADIO DAMASCUS

AFTER THE

ASSASSINATION OF

ANWAR SADAT,

OCTOBER 6, 1981

In the 1970s, after the collapse of the Arab states' efforts on behalf of the Palestinians, the PLO and its various splinter groups became notorious for hijackings and terrorist attacks. In 1970 Yasser Arafat and his guerrillas were expelled from their bases in Jordan after King Hussein began to suspect they were trying to take over the country (which has a majority of Palestinian-descended citizens). They shifted to Lebanon, where their presence helped turn the balance of power away from the dominant Christians and spark a bloody civil war in the mid-'70s. From that point on, the PLO had virtually free reign in southern Lebanese territory and used it to lob rockets into Israel and stage terrorist attacks across Lebanon's border, all organized from its headquarters in Beirut. Israel had already mounted one major incursion into Lebanon to stamp out guerrilla bases in 1978, but that only temporarily forced the guerrillas farther north.

Begin was reelected by a whisker in 1981 in the wake of a successful air force operation that destroyed Iraq's Osirak nuclear reactor, which Israel claimed was approaching weapons-production capacity. It was a major gambit by the crafty leader, but the operation, which was over in about three hours, involved no Israeli casualties and was seen in Israel as just the kind of preemptive move needed in a technologically dangerous world.

Tragically, Sadat was assassinated by Islamic fundamentalists in Egypt only a few months later. Coming on the heels of the fundamentalist takeover in Iran, there were clear signals that a new and dangerous threat to Israel,

A BEATEN MAN

By the summer of 1983, under the strain of the war, Begin seemed to be losing his spirit with each new day, with each new casualty. The proud and defiant prime minister never admitted that he felt Lebanon was a mistake, but in August he suddenly resigned.

to the West, and to peace was taking root in the region.

In 1982 Begin and Defense Minister Ariel Sharon resolved to stamp out the PLO in Lebanon. On June 6 three Israeli divisions rumbled across the Lebanese border through a strip of territory controlled by a friendly Lebanese militia—the South Lebanon Army—and headed due north toward PLO positions. The government intended to move the PLO forces 40 kilometers (25 miles) north of the border—out of rocket range. As expected they achieved this aim within days; the PLO was expelled from the coastal towns of Tyre and Sidon and from the main inland towns and villages of south Lebanon.

At first, most Israelis—even the Labor opposition—stood behind their leaders. After all, Israel's northern towns had lived through more than their share of bombings and terror infiltrations. The army seized tons of materiel from the PLO, including tanks, rockets, antitank weapons, and artillery pieces. Then the Syrian air force, from its own positions in the north and east of the country, proceeded to take on Israel, and they were routed. Israeli troops then continued north. Their plan was to expel the PLO from Beirut, necessitating Israel's first-ever siege of an Arab capital.

In mid-June the air force began pounding Beirut from Israeli positions atop Shuf mountain to the south and from gunboats at sea to the west. With the Lebanese Christians in East Beirut as their allies, the siege was thorough. But it dragged on, doing grievous harm to Israel's international standing and

In the wake of the killing of Lebanese Christian leader Bashir Jemayel, Israel allowed Jemayel's outraged Phalange militia into the Palestinian refugee camps of Sabra and Shatila. The massacre of hundreds of men, women, and children caused an uproar in Israel and throughout the world.

causing considerable damage in Beirut. Even many Israelis began sounding a note of dissent. On July 22, an army colonel, Eli Geva, stunned the nation by requesting he be relieved of his duties in Lebanon because of conscientious objections to the attack on Beirut and the harm done to innocent civilians.

But after two months of heavy action, capped by American mediation, the PLO agreed to leave. On August 21 some 14,000 Palestinian fighters and Syrian troops supporting them began their evacuation. A week later, with Israel's overt encouragement, the Lebanese parliament elected Christian Phalange leader Bashir Jemayel—a friend of Israel's—as the new president of Lebanon. In Israel there were dreams of a peace treaty with the Jemayel-led, PLO-free neighbor to the north. But on September 14 Jemayel was assassinated when a car bomb—responsibility for it later was claimed by Syria—destroyed his headquarters; within hours Israel seized key junctions in West Beirut and allowed the Phalange militia into the Palestinian refugee camps. Despite warnings from Sharon against harming civilians, the militias entered the camps called Sabra and Shatila and murdered hundreds of refugees.

In Israel there was howling protest. Begin was forced to set up an inquiry commission, which several months later found Israel bore indirect responsibility for the killings. This resulted in the ouster of several top military officials and the demotion of Sharon.

STRANGE BEDFELLOWS

In October 1986, Shimon Peres honored his "rotation agreement" and signed over the premiership to Likud leader Yitzhak Shamir. In his two years in power Peres withdrew the army from Lebanon and ended hyperinflation. But the two-headed "unity governments," which served through six years of political stalemate, never managed to agree on what to do about the occupied territories.

LEAVING LEBANON

(opposite) The government led by Labor's Shimon Peres ordered the army out of most of Lebanon. However, Israel remained in control of a buffer zone along the border, which it policed with the help of a Lebanese militia.

These events had a more profound psychological impact: For the first time many Israelis were deeply ashamed of something that their government and military had been involved in. A sense of disillusion regarding Israel's fundamental righteousness grew, and Israelis lost the sense that theirs was a country with moral advantage.

"Whatever its final outcome, the epitaph to be placed upon the war in Lebanon will read: Here lies the international stature and moral integrity of a wonderful people," wrote one observer, Prof. Ze'ev Manowitz, in *Ha'aretz*.

It was, perhaps, all part of a chain of events that Begin himself had set in motion. His 1977 election had heralded a series of free-market reforms in the economy, and his peace agreement with Egypt had raised high hopes. But these events also created the expectation of new levels of peace and prosperity for the country, and as some of those hopes seemed to be fulfilled, Israelis began to think less about the state and more about their individual needs.

But now the military was locked in a mess in Lebanon. The Peace Now group held angry protests against Begin and Sharon; at one of them in Jerusalem, on February 10, 1983, a nationalist youth hurled a grenade into the crowd of protesters, killing peace activist Emil Grinzweig.

Begin eventually resigned in the summer of 1983, offering no explanation save an enigmatic "I cannot go on." He became a recluse and passed away nine years later. He never publicly spoke about his political career or its sad ending, but his passing was met with much introspection. Although his legacy was enigmatic and controversial, many Israelis felt Begin was unique. Even his rivals found him ultimately forgivable.

The occupation of the southern half of Lebanon—which cost hundreds of Israeli and Lebanese lives—ended in 1985. During the previous year a deadlocked Israeli election led to the establishment of a joint Labor-Likud government led by Shimon Peres (who promised to rotate the premiership with Yitzhak Shamir, Begin's successor at the helm of the Likud).

Despite the phased pullout from Lebanon—three years after the invasion—Israel continued to control a border zone in south Lebanon to prevent incursions from a new enemy that arose there: Shiite Muslim Lebanese, primarily the fundamentalist Hezbollah militia, which was backed by Iran.

In addition to the withdrawal from most of Lebanon the "national unity government" also succeeded in ending the hyperinflation that had dogged the economy throughout most of Likud's seven years at the helm and which led to a stock market crash in 1983. An austerity program and a temporary price freeze brought inflation from more than 400 percent a year down to the manageable teens by the mid-1980s. Both moves were achieved by Labor with the support of one Likud minister in the evenly split cabinet; in the case of the Lebanon pullout it was Housing Minister David Levy, and in the case of the economic plan it was Finance Minister Yitzhak Moda'i. But there proved to be no way Labor and Likud could break their fundamental disagreement over the West Bank and Gaza.

Labor had concluded that it was in Israel's strong interest to give up most of these territories in order to avoid becoming, in effect, a binational state as opposed to one predominantly Jewish; the fact that the party viewed the territories as a burden also made it proactive in seeking a solution. Likud, on the other hand, viewed the territories as a net asset and appeared dedicated to retaining them at almost any cost. The party did its best to continue supporting West Bank settlement, which was slowed during the "unity government" years, and paid only lip service to the idea of a peace process with the Palestinians.

eanwhile, the Palestinians were losing patience. On December 9, 1987, what would become known to the world as the Intifada (the "casting off") began because of a car accident that killed a Palestinian youngster in the Gaza Strip. It eventually grew into an open and prolonged conflict, with Israeli soldiers shooting into crowds and engaging in riot actions and occasional gun battles with Palestinians throughout the territories.

The Intifada came as another shock to an Israeli population already spiritually weakened by the war in Lebanon. The small acts of rebellion were initially accepted with some surprise, but as the incidents mounted they quickly led to anger. Finally, as the uprising extended from weeks to months to years and started costing Israeli as well as Palestinian lives, Israelis had to reckon with the idea that there was, perhaps, something fundamentally wrong with the occupation.

Every day Palestinian youths would burn tires on the main roads and throw rocks and bottles at patrolling Israeli soldiers. Palestinians stopped paying taxes, applying for Israeli permits for daily activities, and otherwise cooperating with Israeli authorities. Palestinian policemen working for Israel quit their jobs. Commerce was frequently on strike. Universities were shut down.

THE TERROR CONTINUES

Throughout the '70s and '80s Israel suffered through a series of terrorist attacks, mostly launched by groups associated with the PLO. Below, a hijacked bus is stormed by a special antiterror unit in March 1988 along the desert highway between Beer Sheva and Dimona. The hijackers and several passengers were killed.

INTIFADA

The "Intifada," a fierce popular uprising by Palestinians in the occupied territories, began innocuously with a car accident in the Gaza Strip. Israel was surprised when the clash refused to die down, then spread to the West Bank. Israeli troops found themselves facing constant rioting and danger, and every man, woman, and child was a possible threat—and a possible victim. (left) These soldiers are on a quick patrol through central Hebron.

ALLEYS AND STONES

(right) "The children of the stones" were everywhere during the Intifada, which lasted from December 1987 through the early 1990s. Images like these, of youths throwing stones and burning tires, were, in fact, the hallmark of the uprising.

Israeli troops beat, arrested, shot, and chased Palestinians all over the territories, sometimes searching homes in the middle of the night, arresting people in their pajamas. Throughout Israel this struck many people who were watching it on television as not just absurd but shameful. In all, more than 1,000 Palestinians were killed by Israeli troops during the years of the uprising, and many more were injured.

With another part of their national myth, the so-called 'purity of arms,' being dismantled, active Israeli opposition to the occupation was growing. Dozens of Israelis were refusing army reserve call-ups to serve in the occupied territories. A new slogan was coined at left-wing rallies: "Two states for two peoples." To Shamir, then in his rotation as prime minister, this was unfathomable defeatism, almost treason.

KOLLEK'S JERUSALEM

One of the few mayors to ever become a world figure, Teddy Kollek made Jerusalem his life's project. First elected in 1966, he remained mayor for 27 years and strongly believed in a united Jerusalem as Israel's capital. But he was also a liberal humanist and was seen as a friend to the Arabs. In September 1983 he took Jimmy Carter on a tour of his town.

The 1988 election, held as the territories burned, became a referendum on the question of the Palestinians, and Israelis, apparently thinking a harder line might be the answer, voted in Shamir's coalition of rightist and religious parties; they won 65 of the 120 Knesset seats.

But Shamir, in trying to negotiate coalition agreements, found the religious parties' demands insupportably high. One demand Shamir could simply not bring himself to accept was the requested delegitimization of conversions to Judaism carried out by rabbis of the Reform and Conservative movements. Even though the more liberal Reform and Conservative streams of Judaism were tiny in Israel—just the opposite of the situation in the United States, with its Jewish community just larger than that of Israel at the time—Shamir could not rubber-stamp this Orthodox attempt to strengthen their dominance in Israel.

Shamir invited Labor to join him in another unity government—this time without a rotation. The government lasted less than two years. When it came down, it was because of disagreements about how to launch negotiations with the Palestinians. In the end, Shamir could not bring himself to cross that line.

At the end of the decade, Israel stood on shifting sands, uncertain about its future and increasingly questioning the past and present.

If the '73 war rattled the public's faith that their leaders would do things right, the Lebanon war shattered many people's faith that their government would do the right thing. The army's image as invincible was undermined by its inability to put down the gangs of youths staging the Intifada even while applying sometimes embarrassing brutality against them.

Israelis were also starting to reassess their past, finding out in many cases that it was not as pure or heroic as they had thought. In the late 1980s, at the height of the Palestinian uprising, historian Benny Morris revealed that many if not most of the Arabs known to have "fled" the country during the War of Independence were expelled.

Israel was increasingly ripe for a change.

> *"The sea is the same sea, the Arabs are the same Arabs."*
> **PRIME MINISTER YITZHAK SHAMIR, 1988**

NEVER FORGET

(left) In 1986, Prime Minister Shimon Peres visited the memorial of the Bergen Belsen concentration camp in Germany.

A GRIM ECHO

The case of "Ivan the Terrible," the notoriously sadistic death camp guard at Treblinka, was seen as a sequel to the Eichmann trial. But after he was sentenced to death doubts lingered about whether Ivan Demjanjuk, above, was the right man. The Supreme Court overturned his conviction in 1993, and he returned to the United States amid bitterness on all sides.

> *"Half a million Jews or more who love to learn and read, see theater and go to concerts, people with education. And their children—obedient, polite children, serious and studious. The heart rejoices at the injection of optimism all this will bring to the deteriorating fabric of our society!"*
>
> **COLUMNIST AMNON DANKER,**
>
> **REJOICING AT THE COMING**
>
> **RUSSIAN IMMIGRATION, 1989**

THE RUSSIANS ARE COMING

Anatoly Sharansky, a Soviet mathematician jailed in 1975 for Zionist activities, became a symbol of the plight of millions of Soviet Jews who were forbidden to emigrate. In February 1986, as part of a celebrated spy swap with the United States, Sharansky was released. He received a hero's welcome in Israel upon arriving at Ben-Gurion Airport with his wife, Avital, who had lobbied tirelessly across the world on her husband's behalf.

CHAPTER 6

YEARS OF DECISION

*< The 1990s: A question
of generations, a question of peace,
a question of the nation's soul >*

ROCKET OF HOPE

Israel is one of a handful of nations that has put satellites in orbit. The *Ofek II* scientific satellite was launched in April 1990.

ROCKETS OF FEAR

(opposite) An American-made Patriot missile is launched from the Tel Aviv area on a course to intercept incoming Scuds during the Gulf War. Despite the protective measures, 39 Scuds hit Israeli soil.

In the late summer of 1990 Iraqi leader Saddam Hussein sent his army into neighboring Kuwait in an effort to gain greater control over the Persian Gulf oil supply. No one knew it then, but the chain of events that his power grab unleashed would have vast consequences for Israel.

Remarkably, the trouble surrounding Kuwait did not directly involve the Jewish nation, and the United States wanted it to stay that way as it rallied Israel's Arab rivals and organized a United Nations force in Saudi Arabia to protect the Saudi oil fields. When, in January 1991, the United States made the decision to storm into Kuwait and free it from the Iraqi occupation, it left Israel on the sidelines once again with instructions to keep quiet. Although the war was brief, it nonetheless occasioned one of the most bizarre and frightening episodes in Israel's history, when Saddam launched rockets into Israeli cities.

The Gulf War is remembered in Israel for those few weeks when the threat of Iraqi Scud missiles lurked in the skies while their military sat on its hands, chastened against disrupting the delicate Western-Arab coalition the Bush administration had put together to deal with Hussein. At the height of the attacks Israel's streets were virtually abandoned. People huddled in homes—in basements if they had them—and kept their government-issued gas masks close at hand. There was a real fear that a desperate Iraq would ward off the U.S. troops by launching chemical weapons into Israel.

HIGH NOON IN TEL AVIV

(left) The 1991 Gulf War, in which Israel was not an active participant, nonetheless reminded Israelis how vulnerable their small state was to attack. In a provocative gamble for Arab support in its war with a U.N. alliance led by the United States, Iraq hit Israel with Scud missiles that were feared to contain chemical agents. Deserted streets, gas masks, and an eerie sense of helplessness marked the experience.

A SCUD'S LANDING

(above) One of the Scuds launched into Israel damaged this shopping mall outside Haifa in January 1991.

But if those days of stillness and nights of gas masks were what Israelis remembered most about the conflict, what lingered long after the war were the political cards that were dealt to the various players in its aftermath. It was an extraordinary situation because, for the first time in decades, the United States was involved in a Middle Eastern scenario that was not based solely on anti-Israel sentiment, and one in which it had Arab support for its activities. What side each nation took in the dispute and how it all turned out would have a lasting impact on the balance of power in the region

Jordan and the PLO sided with Iraq, with Jordan doing so tacitly and with restraint, but Yasser Arafat unwisely threw his full weight behind Saddam. When the war ended, with Iraq in deep retreat and the United States victorious, Arafat was left rudderless, and no Arab state could say anything against Israel. The United States moved quickly to exploit Arafat's weakness, Israel's restraint, and Jordan's eagerness to get past its embarrassing support of Iraq. The result was

> "When the first representatives of Israel came to Ethiopia some decades ago, we were surprised to find that all Jews weren't black."
>
> **THE FIRST ETHIOPIAN KNESSET MEMBER, ADISSO MASALLA, 1996**

THE JEWS OF ETHIOPIA

In the second of two airlifts thousands of Ethiopian Jews were brought to Israel in 1991. In "Operation Solomon," the Ethiopians were invited to Israel by the government. Their exact origins unknown, it is believed the Ethiopians were either converted in the Middle Ages or are, in fact, descendants of the original "children of Israel." Their arrival during the Gulf War was unfortunate: They were met at the airport by teams issuing gas masks.

the 1991 Madrid Conference, at which all the parties were brought to the table for the first serious discussions in years.

The Madrid meetings did not lead directly to any breakthroughs. In fact, they were rather infuriating for all the posturing that went on among the various parties and the extreme positions they took. But the talks opened the door to future conversations, in particular peace talks between Israel and Syria, and between Israel and a Palestinian delegation obliged to pretend it did not receive its orders from Arafat.

Meanwhile, Israel was tending to perhaps its last great wave of immigrants. As the communist empire was crumbling, Jews from the former Soviet Union were finally free to follow their hearts—and their pocketbooks—to Israel. From 1990 to 1998, some 800,000 former Soviets immigrated to the Jewish state.

The wave of newcomers had an extraordinary impact on Israel. Not only did many of the Russian Jews bring a cultured, educated background but their arrival—ragged, determined, hopeful, forlorn—brought Israel back to a different time, a time when it had to pull together and take action, to make room for newcomers, to organize and strategize and build more homes and teach Hebrew. For many Israelis, even those who played no role in the absorption efforts and who may have snickered at the bewildered freshmen, there was nonetheless a renewed sense of pride and purpose in the Zionist enterprise. The arrival of these immigrants engendered a sense of hope for all of Israel.

Israel's economy began to expand as a consequence of this tremendous influx. Immigrant engineers began playing a large role in Israel's emergence as a high-tech superpower. Their sheer numbers, and the necessity of feeding, clothing, housing, and providing for them, helped the economy grow at an average of some 5 percent a year through the first half of the decade.

While almost all the newcomers found housing and jobs, not all could be immediately absorbed into their chosen fields, and their adjustment and assimilation to full membership in Israeli society was slow—especially since Israel hoped to avoid the mistake of trying to immediately impose a new culture on immigrants. At the same time, a crop of Russian newspapers, radio stations, and political parties emerged, keeping the new immigrants from more quickly embracing the wider culture. The Russians also had an immediate political impact. Their initial support for the Labor Party would be critical in the 1992 elections.

ABSORPTION

With the collapse of the Soviet Union in 1989, millions of Jews and their families were free to emigrate. Beginning in 1990 more than 800,000 streamed into Israel, bringing with them a major new cultural influence and helping fuel a tremendous economic boom.

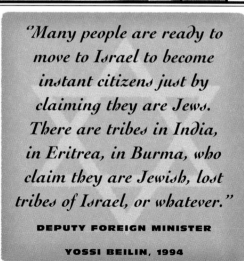

"Many people are ready to move to Israel to become instant citizens just by claiming they are Jews. There are tribes in India, in Eritrea, in Burma, who claim they are Jewish, lost tribes of Israel, or whatever."

DEPUTY FOREIGN MINISTER

YOSSI BEILIN, 1994

With the Madrid Conference opening up a possible path to peace, and the arrival of the Russians, Israel was reaching a turning point. The Palestinian problem in the territories was still festering. There was a growing sense among Israelis that the Likud approach to the Palestinians and the territories was not working, and it seemed that Labor had its best opportunity in years to get back into full command of government. To make the most of the opportunity the party decided to replace Shimon Peres with the far more popular Yitzhak Rabin.

On a June night in 1992, with hope in their hearts, Israel's electorate gave Rabin's dovish coalition 61 of 120 Knesset seats. Standing on the podium in the Knesset before his colleagues and before the nation, with Peres nearby as his foreign minister, Rabin promised an autonomy deal with the Palestinians in less than one year.

Like his predecessors, Rabin at first refused to deal directly with Yasser Arafat's PLO, maintaining the argument that it was a terrorist outfit bent on destroying Israel. But this seemed increasingly weak: First, because the means used by Arafat were hardly a reason for Israel to avoid doing what was in its own interest; and second, because Arafat had been stating for years that his aim was a two-state solution and peace with Israel.

LITTLE RUSSIA

(left) Immigrant housing was fashioned out of empty apartments, unused office space, and low-rent hotels.

CHANGING OF THE GUARD

(below) One day after news of the Oslo accords became public, Yitzhak Rabin spent the afternoon with Army Chief of Staff Ehud Barak, who, in the wake of Rabin's assassination, became head of the Labor Party in 1997. Two decades after retiring from military life, Rabin still cherished his connection to the army, and as prime minister insisted on also serving as defense minister.

Hence in January 1993 the Labor Party led a Knesset motion abolishing the law that forbade Israeli contact with the PLO. Soon after, secret contacts with the PLO began in Oslo, Norway. At first they were led by academics and later by middle-level officials. By the spring of '93 the Oslo talks were being supervised by Foreign Minister Peres and Arafat's number two man, Abu Mazen.

The Palestinian autonomy accord signed at the White House in September 1993 was nicknamed "Gaza and Jericho First," but it included much more. It committed Israel to a second phase of pullouts that would extend Palestinian autonomy to include all of the West Bank except Jewish settlements, army bases, and undefined "security areas." And the sides pledged themselves to a permanent settlement in which the Palestinians expected to receive their own independent state.

For Arafat it was a moment of bliss. Not only were the Palestinians' rights being recognized—in a path that he believed could lead them to his lifetime goal of independence—but he was finally recognized as their leader, a terrorist no longer. For Arafat, who had been kicked out of Beirut like a bandit after Israel's 1982 invasion, this recognition was sweet indeed. Rabin, meanwhile, was uncertain whether to shake Arafat's hand—his former tormentor seemed somehow too eager. He later said he had butterflies in his stomach at the very prospect. But in the end, with President Clinton gently easing him on, Rabin did reach out.

But the hopes for a quick peace were dashed.

On the very day the agreement was being signed in Washington, Islamic fundamentalists of the Hamas group killed eight Israeli soldiers on patrol in Gaza. Through the fall dozens more Israelis were killed in attacks throughout the country. In December a Jewish settler named Mordechai Lapid and one of his children were gunned down near Hebron. As they died they were cradled by a neighbor, Brooklyn-born physician Dr. Baruch Goldstein, a deeply observant Jew. Two months after, still unable to manage his anger and despair, Goldstein visited Hebron's revered Tomb of the Patriarchs. Armed with a submachinegun, he walked into the mosque inside the castlelike structure and began firing at the worshippers, killing 29 Arab villagers. Dozens more died by the fire of Israeli troops in riots that erupted in the territories.

Hamas vowed revenge attacks. The first came in April 1994, when a car exploded near a bus in the northern Israeli town of Afula, killing eight Israelis. It established a grisly precedent: Some 200 Israelis were killed over the next two years in similar attacks, mostly suicide bombings. The peace process,

> *"I, military I.D. number 30743, retired general of the Israel Defense Forces, consider myself to be a soldier in the army of peace today....We are embarking on a battle which has no dead and no wounded, no blood and no anguish. This is the only battle which is a pleasure to wage: the battle for peace."*
>
> **YITZHAK RABIN, FAILING TO FORESEE HIS ASSASSINATION IN HIS SPEECH TO CONGRESS, JULY 1994**

A HISTORIC HANDSHAKE

Even as he stood on the podium with Bill Clinton and Yasser Arafat, it is not clear whether Yitzhak Rabin really expected to shake hands with the Palestinian leader. A gently encouraging Clinton urged the two men together. In Israel, where the event kept millions riveted to the TV, the handshake was truly shocking, a sign that peace was serious.

unfortunately, did not bring the Israelis the security they had long sought.

In July 1994 King Hussein of Jordan stepped forward, announcing to his people on Jordanian TV that he would meet Rabin in Washington in a few days. The meeting was a success, and the next day, standing before Congress, Hussein simply said: "The state of war between Israel and Jordan is over." Rabin, in one of his most moving speeches, described himself as "a soldier in the army of peace...embarking on a battle which has no dead and no wounded, no blood and no anguish."

It was a culmination of decades of flirtation between Israel and Jordan. Hussein's grandfather, Abdullah, had sought accommodation with Israel. Historians now say that during the 1948 war, Abdullah even had a tacit agreement with Israel to avoid an invasion of its vulnerable, narrow coast, and was merely to take over the West Bank, which had already been earmarked by the U.N. for the Palestinian Arab state.

Western-educated and moderate, Hussein spent most of his rule trying to reach a quiet understanding with Israel. He met with its leaders—even with Shamir—in secret many times. But his favorite was Rabin, the tough old soldier-turned-peacemaker. The two developed a gentle affection for each other fueled by the fact that Hussein sought not the cold peace that Egypt had given Israel but a true partnership. When he warmly spoke of peace between "the children of Abraham," Israelis saw his eyes glistening, and he won their hearts.

The peace process was nothing short of an economic booster rocket for Israel. The Arab League annulled most aspects of the boycott, which opened previously unknown export markets for Israel and allowed companies from around the world to do business with Israel without fear of losing the poorer—but vast—Arab market. There was also a flood of foreign investment in the country because of the feeling that it was headed toward stability.

NEW OLD FRIENDS

When Jordan's King Hussein met Rabin at the White House for a formal declaration of non-belligerency, the two men were genuine friends. On opposite sides of the 1967 war that put Jerusalem in the hands of Israel, 30 years later the two adversaries shared a common sense of destiny. Hussein's dignity and panache made him an instant favorite of the Israeli people.

In October 1994, a terrorist opposed
to the peace process blew himself up
on a No. 5 bus in Tel Aviv. Twenty-one
people were killed. The blast was the
first in a series of suicide bombings
carried out by Islamic fundamentalist
radicals who succeeded in shaking
Israelis' faith in peace.

Exports grew 52 percent between 1992 and 1995; foreign investments grew
tenfold, from about $200 million a year before Rabin to more than $2 billion
in 1995; tourist arrivals doubled to more than 2 million a year. Defense
expenditures fell dramatically to about 7 percent of GDP. Israeli trade missions
toured the Arab world, from Morocco to Kuwait, sizing up possible investments
and joint ventures. Deals on regional railways, importing natural gas from the
Gulf, and joint industrial parks were discussed. In the years 1990–1996 Israel's
economy grew by a combined 48 percent, with the greatest per capita growth
by far coming in 1994–95, at the height of Rabin's peacemaking. As a result,
Israelis attained a per capita income of about $17,000, comparable to the middle
range of countries in the European Union.

This coincided with the onset of commercial and cable TV in Israel—the
spearhead of an unprecedented openness to the world, especially to the West.
Many of the top American TV shows found their way to Israeli stations. Scores
of first-run American movies played every night in the cities. Many of the top
American food and commercial chains set up shop in the Jewish state.

But this meant little to the people who saw the abandonment of the West
Bank as a betrayal of the age-old Jewish cause; some, in fact, feared the foreign
influence as decadent.

In the fall of 1995, the government signed a deal with the Palestinians detailing the expansion of the autonomy set up in 1994 in Gaza and the West Bank City to Jericho. Within months all the cities of the West Bank would have full autonomy, and the villages where almost all the rest of the Arab population lived would come under Palestinian civilian control.

Extreme-right rabbis ruled that it was forbidden for the army to dismantle bases or otherwise partake in a withdrawal from the West Bank. Some even argued that Rabin was an "oppressor of Jews," implying that under ancient Jewish law he deserved death. During at least one mass rally protesters waved posters depicting Rabin in a Nazi SS uniform. On several occasions the cars of cabinet ministers were attacked by mobs. Security chief Carmi Gilon warned that Rabin and the cabinet were in danger and futilely urged Rabin to wear a security vest during all public appearances.

In secret, cabinet minister Yossi Beilin, architect of the Oslo talks, was reaching a deal with Abu Mazen whereby in a final peace settlement the Palestinian autonomy would be upgraded to a state in Gaza and most of the West Bank.

PUSHING FOR THEOCRACY

The ultra-Orthodox in Israel, who numbered some half million, transformed through the years from a relatively docile and spiritually separatist segment of society into a serious political movement. In 1994 they protested archaeological digs that they felt were disturbing ancient Jewish burial grounds. They also frequently protested the "desecration" of the Jewish Sabbath.

THE VIOLENCE GROWS

For many religious and right-wing Israelis the prospect of giving away the heartland of biblical Israel was an unmitigated disaster and a blasphemy. They made the peace process their number one issue and Rabin their number one enemy, staging violent protests and bringing internal conflict to a reinvigorated level of aggression and recrimination. (top) A demonstration in 1993.

WHITHER THE GOLAN?

"Peace with the Golan" was the slogan of Israelis who opposed Rabin's willingness to trade the Golan Heights, captured in 1967, for peace with Syria. (above) The sign, here on the rolling plateau of the Golan itself, also hung from many balconies in Israel's cities. The campaign was very popular, and in the end the Rabin and Peres governments did not strike the deal.

CROSSING THE LINE

(right) Rabin's lifelong image as a warrior and a patriot was essential in helping him sell the peace accords. The right-wing made an effort to undermine this image with personal attacks against him.

NETANYAHU EMERGES

Articulate, American-educated Benjamin Netanyahu swept to the leadership of the Likud Party in the spring of 1993. In September, as a majority of Israelis welcomed the dawn of a new era of hope, Netanyahu—in the streets and in the Knesset—excoriated the agreements with the PLO as a sellout of Jewish rights to the land and as a disaster for national security.

DEATH TO RABIN

On July 2, 1994, the day Yasser Arafat returned to Gaza after 25 years in exile, Netanyahu led an angry protest by tens of thousands of West Bank settlers and others. From the balcony in Jerusalem's Zion Square, where he spoke, hung a sign that said "Death to Arafat"—but many in the crowd also chanted "Death to Rabin." Afterward, some of the demonstrators rampaged through the Old City, destroying Arab property.

The Government of the State of Israel and the P.L.O. team (in the Jordanian-Palestinian delegation to the Middle East Peace Conference) (the "Palestinian Delegation"), representing the Palestinian people, agree that it is time to put an end to decades of confrontation and conflict, recognize their mutual legitimate and political rights, and strive to live in peaceful coexistence and mutual dignity and security and achieve a just, lasting, and comprehensive peace settlement and historic reconciliation through the agreed political process.

FROM THE "DECLARATION OF PRINCIPLES ON INTERIM SELF-GOVERNMENT ARRANGEMENTS,"

FORMALLY SIGNED IN WASHINGTON, SEPTEMBER 13, 1993

Peace is hereby established between the State of Israel and the Hashemite Kingdom of Jordan (the "Parties") effective from the exchange of the instruments of ratification of this Treaty.

The Parties will apply between them the provisions of the Charter of the United Nations and the principles of international law governing relations among states in times of peace.

FROM THE

"TREATY OF PEACE BETWEEN THE STATE OF ISRAEL AND THE HASHEMITE KINGDOM OF JORDAN,"

SIGNED ON THE ISRAEL-JORDAN BORDER IN THE ARAVA VALLEY, OCTOBER 26, 1994

*"The government of Israel
announces with astonishment,
great sorrow, and deep grief
the death of Yitzhak Rabin,
who was murdered by
an assassin."*

RABIN AIDE EYTAN HABER,

NOVEMBER 4, 1995

ragedy struck on November 4, as Rabin was leaving a triumphant rally
in Tel Aviv where 100,000 people had turned out to cheer his peace policies.
As he was about to enter his car, Yigal Amir, a religious 25-year-old law
student and active supporter of the settlers, reached through Rabin's
bodyguards and shot him twice in the back with a Beretta 9-millimeter
handgun. Rabin was rushed to nearby Ichilov Hospital. An hour and a half
later, Rabin's loyal aide Eytan Haber emerged from the hospital gates to read
a short statement: "The government of Israel announces with astonishment,
great sorrow, and deep grief the death of Yitzhak Rabin, who was murdered
by an assassin."

Israel—and the world—was deep in grief. Rabin, an essentially
uncommunicative man and an extreme and sometimes plodding pragmatist,
had appeared to have undergone a spiritual transformation during his last
years. Now, in death his image softened even more, and in the minds of Israelis
he became the very embodiment of peace, of hope, of light, of tranquillity.
They turned him into a prophet and they mourned him as a saint. Thousands
of children streamed to the square where he was gunned down, burning
candles through the night and strumming folk songs on guitars. Many right-
wing Israelis felt chastened, and Israelis of every stripe vowed to be more
moderate. Soon, polls would show that for the first time in years Labor was
far ahead of Likud in public opinion.

The Labor Party chose Peres to succeed Rabin. In the weeks after
the assassination Peres marched forward with the Oslo plan, withdrawing
Israeli troops from all the major West Bank cities except Hebron,
which was to be last because it had a Jewish community living in
its downtown, creating a complicated situation.

In January the Palestinians held an election that made Arafat
their formal leader and yielded a parliament. But an event with
probably greater implications came when Hamas bomb maker
Yehiya Ayyash was killed by an exploding mobile phone.
Nicknamed "The Engineer," Ayyash had masterminded most of the
Hamas bombings of the previous several years, earning him the
number one spot on Israel's most wanted list. Israel did not claim
responsibility for the attack—as has always been its policy—but
Hamas vowed that with or without "The Engineer," there would be
revenge attacks. Ignoring this, Peres decided a few weeks later to
hold in May the election initially scheduled for November.

The stage was set for an electoral confrontation that for the first time would pit a representative of the founding generation against an Israeli born after the state: opposition leader Benjamin Netanyahu, whose brother was killed at Entebbe. In 1993 Netanyahu defeated a battery of Likud veterans in an internal election and succeeded Shamir as the head of the party. As opposition leader Netanyahu adopted a far-right ideology, attacking the Oslo Accords as a disaster that placed Israel's security in the hands of an arch-terrorist, and blaming Arafat for the Hamas bombings. He was an articulate and effective enemy of the peace process.

Things started to fall apart for Peres on February 25, when a bomb ripped through a bus on Route 18 near Jerusalem's central bus station, killing 26 people, including the suicide bomber. Peres grimly visited the site surrounded by bodyguards and watched as ultra-Orthodox volunteers went through their grisly ritual of picking up pieces of flesh and torn limbs and placing them into small nylon bags for proper Jewish burial.

About an hour later another man carrying explosives strapped around his waist drove up to a soldiers' hitchhiking station at a crossroads near the southern city of Ashkelon and blew himself up, killing a female soldier. A week later another militant blew himself up on a bus in Jerusalem, killing 18 people,

A NATION GRIEVES

Rabin's burial drew scores of world leaders, including an unprecedented turnout from the Arab world. In a day awash with images, the most memorable was this one of Rabin's family. Granddaughter Noa Ben-Artzi, pictured here to the right of widow Leah Rabin, moved the world with the eulogy in which she remembered "my hero."

I was a soldier for 27 years.

I fought as long as there was no prospect for peace. I believe that now there is a chance for peace. A great chance. Which must be seized.

Violence is undermining the foundations of Israeli democracy. It must be rejected and condemned. And it must be contained. It is not the way of the state of Israel. Democracy is our way. There may be differences, but they will be resolved in democratic elections...

There is no painless way forward for Israel, but the way of peace is preferable to the way of war. And I am speaking as a military man, as a minister of defense, who sees the pain of the families of the soldiers of the Israel Defense Forces. It is for their sake, for the sake of our children and grandchildren, that I want this government to exhaust every tiny possibility to move ahead and reach a comprehensive peace.

This demonstration must send a message to the Israeli public, to the Jews of the world, to the multitudes in the Arab lands, and to the world at large: The nation of Israel wants peace, supports peace.

And for this, I thank you all.

YITZHAK RABIN, SPEAKING TO A PEACE RALLY AT KINGS OF ISRAEL SQUARE IN TEL AVIV,

NOVEMBER 4, 1995, JUST AN HOUR BEFORE HE WAS ASSASSINATED

including several foreign workers from Romania. The next day a Palestinian man got off a truck that had smuggled him from Gaza, approached the Dizengoff Center shopping mall, and pressed the button that sent a tiny spark to the TNT he carried in his shoulder bag; 14 people—half of them children—were killed, and more than 100 were injured.

Netanyahu's campaign rang true. In his TV ads his slogan was: "There is no peace. There is no security. There is no reason to vote for Peres."

It was the first election in which the prime minister was elected directly, and there was a second ballot for the Knesset parties. Peres, his message of hope crushed by the terrorist attacks, lost by less than one percent.

Beyond its impact on the peace process, the '96 election also showed that a new social and political reality was emerging in Israel. Instead of having two big blocs dominated by Labor and Likud, the Knesset turned into an array of midsized parties strongly linked to sectarian groups within Israel's society, indicating clearly where the future fault lines lay. Labor's vote was overwhelmingly Ashkenazi. Likud's was mostly Sephardi. Many Russian immigrants voted for a Russian party headed by former "refusenik" Natan (Anatoly) Sharansky. Israel's one million Arab citizens voted mostly for Arab parties. Most remarkable, perhaps, was the resurgence of the religious parties, who won a record 23 of the Knesset's 120 seats. And the religious revival was coalescing with Sephardi separatism; the ultra-Orthodox Shas party won 10 seats, getting a vote from one in five Sephardi Jews.

THE EXECUTIONER

Assassin Yigal Amir was brought to the renamed "Rabin Square" in the dead of night to reenact his deed. Throughout his trial the unrepentant Amir maintained that Rabin had been a traitor and sought to redefine the killing in terms of divine judgment. "He was executed," Amir would say.

By the mid-1990s, on the eve of its 50th anniversary, Israel had turned away from its founders. It elected a prime minister who was younger than the state itself, and it dropped, in fear, the peace process that Rabin and Peres had worked for. On the verge of 50 Israel turned away from the men who were there at the beginning—who hitchhiked with Ben-Gurion as teenagers before the state's birth, who blazed the trail to Jerusalem in the War of Independence, who built Israel's military, who masterminded the Six Day War, who had saved the economy from collapse in the 1980s, and who finally, with the special moral authority and vision that was theirs alone, brought Israel to the brink of peace with its Arab neighbors.

On the eve of its 50th birthday, with Rabin gone and Peres rejected, a dispirited Israel turned away from the past, and, uncertain of the future, pressed hard on the gas.

A NEW GENERATION

In May 1996, seven months after Rabin's murder, the Labor Party suffered a shocking and narrow defeat at the polls. A wave of terrorist suicide bombings in Israel's cities had unsettled many Israelis, and despite Rabin's legacy, a new prime minister with a far different agenda assumed the helm. Benjamin Netanyahu was the first Israeli prime minister younger than the state itself.

"MR. PERES, IT'S NOT ENOUGH TO BE PHOTOGRAPHED WITH KIDS— YOU HAVE TO PROTECT THEM." LIKUD CANDIDATE BENJAMIN NETANYAHU, TV DEBATE ON MAY 26, 1996

LAYERS OF TIME

Five thousand years of history, one unifying thread.

STORY WITHOUT END

< The last 50 years were but brush strokes on a larger canvas >

Some 5,000 years ago, they say, a man named Abraham walked the hills of Judea. They say he was the father of the Jewish nation, and of Judaism.

Some 2,000 years ago, they say, a man named Jesus walked this same patch of earth. His words spawned the Christian idea and changed the world.

Some 1,400 years ago, they say, a man named Mohammed came to this land, too. They say that from a hilltop in Jerusalem, he ascended to heaven on a great winged stallion. His teachings gave birth to Islam.

WHERE IT ALL BEGAN

The Tomb of the Patriarchs in Hebron, reputed burial place of Abraham.

LAND OF THE BIBLE

(opposite) Megiddo, where the Bible says that the last, decisive battle between good and evil will take place.

PLATEAU OF SACRIFICE

Masada, where nearly 1,000 Jews took their lives rather than be captured by Romans in the first century.

LAND OF KINGS

Vestiges of a grand Roman settlement at Caesaria.

In these small hills, in this one place, the three great monotheistic religions were born—and each would go on to have a major impact far beyond these hills, changing human codes of thought and action. Storied empires would rise and fall, touched by the ripples of the lives of these three men; legendary monuments would be built, destroyed, and rebuilt; nations would engage in great centuries-long battles that transformed the development of civilization; and vast stores of knowledge would be recorded in their names, passed down through the generations, hidden, protected, scorned, and exalted. Much of the history of Western civilization was born on this sliver of land situated between the Jordan River and the Mediterranean Sea—the place, they say, God called the Land of Israel.

The relics of the generations are still there: the tomb in Hebron, where the Bible tells us Abraham lays buried; the stone wall that once formed a foundation of the great Jewish Temple in Jerusalem; the crumbling yet still distinguishable remnants of the Babylonian, Roman, and Ottoman empires that

successively conquered the region; the narrow alley where the New Testament tells us Jesus bore the cross; the fragile papyrus scrolls that confirm the origins of the Bible itself; and the rock from whence Mohammed took flight into legend. For any child reared in one of the three monotheistic religions, this is the place of record. For any student of Western history, civilization, law, literature, or faith, this is a place of origins.

But for the Jewish people the great chords of time and circumstance that bind them to this land and its history are of a different nature. As a people they were molded from this soil many thousands of years ago, and since that time they have been the sole constant in the story of this land, the sole flower of today's world, whose roots extend across the layers of time to a man called Abraham, to a covenant with God, to the starting place of a story without end.

Not even *Fiddler on the Roof* ran that long. But just as fictional Tevye clung to the traditions of his ancient family and his faith in a world swirling with change, so have generation upon generation of Jewish communities throughout the world.

What makes the last 50 years of Jewish history so interesting is not that they were the most recent 50, or even that they were the first 50 of the modern state called Israel. No, what makes these last 50 years stand out, in a history 100 times that length, is that in these 50 years, for the first time in two millennia, the main characters have come full circle. They have returned, the same but different, to a home that is also both familiar yet strange. No longer must they turn to one another at the Passover seder, wistful and self-conscious, and proclaim: "Next year, in Jerusalem!" Now Jerusalem is part of their daily lives, not a distant aspiration but a reality.

But what about next year in Jerusalem? Where will the story go from here?

It is a nagging kind of question, for even after Herzl's dream came true, even after Hebrew was revived from ancient scrolls of Torah, even after 50 years of struggle, growth, enrichment, and survival, Israel must still come to grips with enormous questions of nationhood. The next 50 years will not simply be a further unfolding of developing circumstances. They will be a time of reckoning. For there are too many unanswered questions, delayed decisions, and simmering issues from the first 50 years of the state that demand it.

FLIGHTS OF THE SPIRIT

Mount Tabor, where Jesus was
transfigured in the presence of
his apostles.

Everyone knows that Jerusalem is the focal point of an unresolved, epic tug-of-war between the Israelis and the Palestinians, between Jews and Arabs, between Judaism and Islam.

What is less well-known is that Jerusalem is one of Israel's poorest cities. Its residents are made up largely of the Orthodox and ultra-Orthodox religious, government bureaucrats, Arabs of different groups and religions, and students and drifters from around the world. Like Washington, D.C., the sparkle and shine of government buildings and investment and the constant flow of tourists make Jerusalem seem more prosperous than it really is. And yet one thing has been the immovable foundation beneath its past and the sturdy, unfailing strength of its present: It is an irresistible magnet of—and for—people.

Perhaps no other place in Israel serves as a more fundamental mirror of society than Jerusalem's Mahane Yehuda produce market. In its undistinguished alleys and sheds, in its bunkerlike stalls, all of Israel is on display: The most religious of Jews move through in dark flannel coats and black hats and beards; secular Jews come in jeans and white T-shirts; Arabs— Muslim, Christian, Druze, and an occasional Bedouin—offer produce, breads,

A VAULT OF HEAVEN

(above) Christian pilgrims in the Judean desert.

THE SAMARITAN WAY

(opposite) The Samaritans, as the sun rises over the Galilee. They are a tiny community of several hundred who consider themselves the original Israelis.

and trinkets for sale; young Palestinians push hand trucks with crates of watermelons, avocados, and cucumbers. The wealthy and the poor and the middle class run together here, as do the Ashkenazi and Sephardi Jews. Soldiers in green fatigues, men and women, students from yeshivas and nearby Hebrew University, government workers, ministers, journalists, merchants, and businesspeople all pass through within the span of any few minutes. In this one market, like in great central markets the world over, one can feel fleeting moments of togetherness and human harmony that national myths strive so relentlessly to create.

Israel is no exception in the mythmaking department. Beneath the surface of its nation-building efforts it has, to one degree or another, either largely ignored, pretended to have overcome, or halfheartedly grappled with three considerable social stress fractures. One causes quiet pain in the relationship between Israel's one million Arab citizens and the larger Jewish citizenry. Another hobbles the sense of unity and equality between Israel's Ashkenazi and Sephardi Jews. And the third, the role of religion in the state, is slowly, insistently driving a chisel into the bedrock of the nation's soul, splitting the religious from the secular, the Orthodox from the liberal. Behind each of these social fractures lies the tense question of the nation's self-determination. Just what kind of place do the Jews want their homeland to become?

Numbering about one million, the Arabs of Israel live mostly in the medium to small towns of the country's interior, or in small enclaves adjacent to larger Jewish cities, remaining out of sight for most of the country's Jews. These are the Arabs who either by choice or fate ended up within the confines of the newly formed Jewish state following the 1948 War of Independence. After the war about 150,000 remained, accounting for more than one in six Israelis.

Stunningly, the Arabs have kept up and even slightly increased their proportion even though the Jewish segment of society has grown by wave upon wave of immigrants, by millions of newcomers from all over the world. And even though the much higher Israeli Arab birthrate is falling, it remains almost twice as high as that of the Jews. Before the birthrates even out, the Israeli Arabs will very likely form a quarter of the population, perhaps more.

The Arabs in Israel actually comprise a variety of different groups. The majority are Muslim, and they live mainly in the northern Galilee region and in several clusters of communities such as the Triangle area in the center of the country. The Christian Arabs—about one in 10—live in scattered enclaves throughout the country, with a large population in Nazareth, where there are numerous Christian institutions. The Druze are a different sect, living mostly in the north. And the tens of thousands of Bedouin, with their secretive, still partly nomadic lifestyle, live mostly in the Negev Desert and in the south.

The Druze and the Bedouin have had the easiest time adjusting to and being accepted by the Jewish majority. Many even serve in the army, gaining fame, in particular, as trackers.

Despite the fact that through the years the Muslims and the Christians have remained largely silent, quietly sitting out the Arab-Israeli conflict, contributing to the economy from the fringe, mastering Hebrew as a second language, and taking each small gain in stride, and despite their apparent willingness to grow into the larger framework of society, they have been kept to the margins. In the 1960s the Military Administration watching over their communities was lifted, but within the Jewish mind there remain doubts about whether the Arabs can truly be Israeli without changing Israel completely.

Still, the Arabs know they have accepted this situation as a bearable necessity of living in a stable, prospering environment. Many families live in the same houses that were originally built by their forebears centuries ago. But their willingness to accept their status, to remain invisible, is already disappearing. For the first time there is talk of fielding an Arab candidate for prime minister in the next election.

When some sort of external peace with neighboring Arab states has been secured, Israel's focus will turn inward, and one group waiting near the front of the line will be the Israeli Arabs, who for already more than 50 years have been silent partners in the Israeli enterprise.

For many Israelis, however, the issue that hit closer to home was the lingering divide between Ashkenazi and Sephardi Jews.

It is a divide that dates back to the immigration wave in the early years of the state, when Jews from Middle Eastern countries first began to arrive en masse into the state that was created in the image of the European Jews who had made it their project. It has always been assumed that the problem would eventually melt away by virtue of an "intermarriage" rate estimated at around a quarter of all unions.

And indeed, a majority of Israel's Sephardi-descended Jews have become, in some way, culturally integrated into an amalgamated "Israeliness." But there is still a large group who are largely estranged from the mainstream, essentially Western flow of society. And public opinion surveys on almost every issue, election results, economic data, and anecdotal evidence reveal that there are still, to a surprising degree, two Jewish peoples living in Israel.

Herzl himself had hoped the Jewish state would have a European character, would be "a portion of a rampart of Europe against Asia, an outpost of civilization as opposed to barbarism." Many believe the country must be Western in its culture (the sound of the music, the feel of the movies, the pulse of the street) if it is to be advanced in its economy and enlightened in its society. Yet even as the country becomes ever more Americanized in its commerce and in its social habits, there are increasing signs of a Sephardi backlash, and there is a creeping awareness that the societal preference of one type of culture over another must end.

It is the religious divide within Israel, however, that has the potential to undermine its unity and resolve—perhaps even break the state down into civil war, as many Israelis believed was possible following the assassination of Yitzhak Rabin by a religious right-wing extremist.

For Israel's first two decades the religious movements played a relatively small role in national political and social life. Only with the acquisition of the biblical heart of ancient Israel in the 1967 war did a messianic character emerge within mainstream religious institutions.

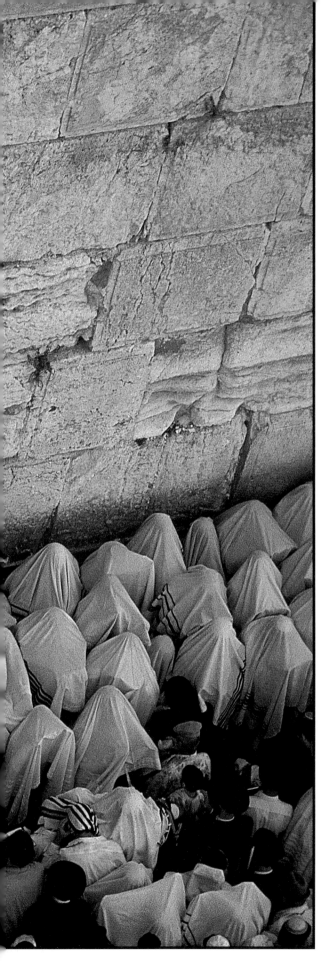

PRIESTLY BLESSING

(left) The Western Wall on the Jewish holiday of Sukkot.

PAPER AND STONE

(right) People come from all over the world to stuff prayers into the cracks of the ancient wall.

CENTURIES OF RESPECT

(below) Father and son at the Western Wall in Jerusalem.

And from that time Israel has become increasingly divided—politically, socially, morally, intellectually—over the future of the state. The fundamental question has been what to do with the West Bank and (to a lesser extent) the Gaza Strip.

Israelis on the "left" would give up all or most of these lands. Some because they believe that this would constitute justice for the Palestinians; many others because they consider the territories, with a large and hostile population, more a burden than an asset. There is also a somewhat paradoxical "Zionist" argument to support this: An Israel that includes the West Bank and Gaza—with the addition

of the Israeli Arab citizens—is 40 percent Arab and growing, and thus simply not a Jewish state. Annexing the territories, thereby extending the democratic right to vote to the Palestinians, would only formalize this.

Israelis on the "right" reach the opposite conclusion. They argue that Israel without the West Bank is indefensibly small, that the Arabs already have some 20 states, and that Israel's moral claim to the West Bank is no less important than its claim to any other part of the Jews' historical homeland, like the area around Tel Aviv.

But increasingly this rightist side of the divide has been powered by those possessed of a religious zeal that sees the land where biblical figures trod as virtually holy in itself—worth dying for not just to carve out a place under the sun (as the early Zionists believed) but to please God (which they most emphatically did not).

As a result of the Labor Party government of 1992–1996, Israel and the Palestinians have embarked on a road that will likely lead to some sort of partition of the country. Despite the election of the more conservative Netanyahu in 1996, the questions now appear to be where the boundary will run and what degree of independence the Palestinians will have. Still unresolved is the fate of the Jews who have settled deep inside the territories— an issue which not only creates a sticky political situation with the Arabs but also reflects a deep spiritual divide between secular and religious Jews about their country's destiny.

Thus, as Israel has handed over authority in the West Bank and Gaza to the Palestinians, many secular Israelis have grown increasingly bitter over the expense of guarding, subsidizing, and otherwise supporting groups of religious Jews who insist on their right to pray at "holy sites" in hostile Palestinian cities: the Tomb of the Patriarchs in Hebron; Joseph's Tomb in Nablus; Rachel's Tomb abutting Bethlehem; and ancient synagogues in Jericho; the village of Halhoul; and other places.

On a more fundamental level, the differences over religion segue into another whole set of issues in the social and personal domain. The passion of belief that fuels that struggle over the land also extends into the social sphere, raising basic questions about who is more Jewish, who has the clearer moral authority, who is working on behalf of centuries of Jewish history and God's will.

If you don't believe in fighting for Hebron, the religious say, what do you believe in? And if what you believe in is so neutral to Judaism, why be here at all? What makes you Jewish other than Judaism? These are tough questions for secular Jews, who have felt no need to defend or explain their Jewishness in the past and are finding that they are increasingly being asked to do so.

A TIME TO LAUGH

Children celebrate on the holiday

of Purim.

Residents in overwhelmingly secular Tel Aviv grumble because a new mall, bought by an ultra-Orthodox millionaire, will now be closed on the Sabbath; they see it as a sign of creeping theocracy. The Orthodox agitate for closing roads near their homes on the Sabbath; the secular must now drive out of the way or face a hail of stones. A planned and funded ultra-Orthodox invasion of a secular neighborhood is soon followed by demands for a more religious lifestyle in the place, and a secular mobilization to keep greater numbers of religious Jews from moving in. Arguments regularly arise between neighbors over observance of the Sabbath. Ultra-Orthodox Jews, many of whom oppose the very existence of the state, refuse to stand still, along with the rest of the country, during an annual siren in memory of Israel's war dead; the secular see this as a crass provocation. Religious youth by the tens of thousands avoid military service by exploiting a draft exemption initially intended for a few hundred seminary students.

To preserve support of religious parties no government has ever challenged Ben-Gurion's decision to give draft exemptions to students of ultra-Orthodox Jewish seminaries, but there is growing secular anger against what has become an obvious incentive for mass draft evasion (in 1996, 28,550 students received the exemption, a figure that accounted for six percent of the potential inductees into the army, according to the newspaper *Ha'aretz*). To stay out of the army these people must remain students for years, forswearing a place in the economy as well. Then they and their families must be supported by the state, even as they refuse to defend it. The result is poverty and dependency among the ultra-Orthodox, and anger and bitterness among the secular majority.

Similarly, no government has reversed Ben-Gurion's decision to give an Orthodox Jewish rabbinate a monopoly over marriage, divorce, and other issues for Jews. One result: a long list of people who are "nonmarriable" because of obscure Orthodox restrictions.

And now there is increasing conflict between the Orthodox and the more liberal streams of Judaism—Conservative and Reform—who are trying to carve out a place for themselves in Israel as, essentially, American imports. Demonstrations have turned ugly and violent, and the words employed come from the lexicon of conflict, not brotherliness.

Are these giant issues? Perhaps not in and of themselves. But as the list grows, as the questions and slights and recriminations become ever more harsh, and as people become increasingly hurt, entrenched, determined, and defensive, society grows apart.

This is not what Israel's founders envisioned. The key individuals and organizations that conceived and led the establishment of the state intended there to be a constitution, with guaranteed individual liberties and, to at least some degree, separation between religion and state. Herzl himself was very clear on these points, and in the wake of the Holocaust it seemed that a strong, free state protective of the Jewish people but inwardly open to their differing interpretations of Judaism would be the ideal place for the Jews to recover and thrive. But there is no constitution because of religious opposition to it.

A HERO OF ISRAEL

The grave of Yitzhak Rabin in Jerusalem.

From the beginning Israel was a land of lofty—perhaps too lofty—aspirations. Not merely content with a straightforward nationalist enterprise, the founders of Zionism wanted to build a model society. They truly wanted to be a "light unto the nations." They wanted to show that the Jews could do better, particularly after the Holocaust.

Despite the deviations from the original plans, the imperfections, and the growing self-doubt, Israel at 50 is one of the truly remarkable success stories of the post–World War II era. In their small, constantly buffeted state on the end of the Mediterranean Sea, the Jewish people have indeed recovered and thrived.

As the 20th century dawned over this land there was virtually no element yet in place of the state and society that exists here today. Now, as the 21st century approaches, the sun rises each day over a land completely transformed.

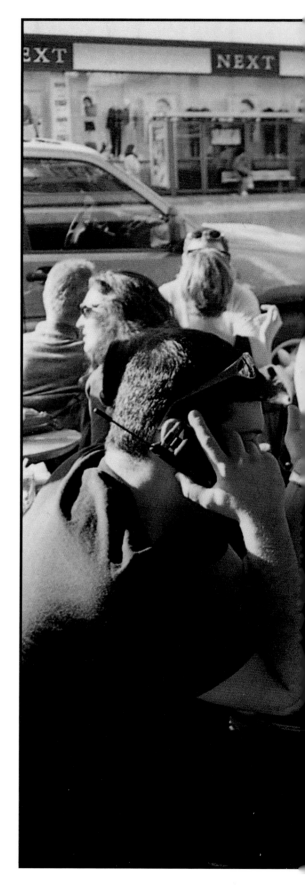

OLD ISRAEL

Selling eggs the old-fashioned way in
Tel Aviv.

YOUNG ISRAEL

The café crowd along Ibn Gvirol Street
in Tel Aviv.

As the dawn creeps across the Golan's high plateau, a uniquely Israeli day
unfolds. As its rays settle into the hills and valleys of the Galilee, the ancient
town of Safed is already wide awake, its artists colony and community of
spiritual mystics rising early to converse with nature; the light traces along
the northern border, where it finds the residents of Kibbutz Misgav Am, "a
kibbutz at the end of the world," still purposefully planted right up against
the barbwire fence with Lebanon, claiming every inch of soil up to the
border. In Jerusalem, the morning color settles down the sides of stone
walls, old and new, with the dancing silence of a falling leaf, then splashes
down into the central plain and southern desert, washing across a surprising
diversity of seaside resorts, suburban enclaves of Volvos and red-tiled roofs,
worn-looking towns on the edge of nowhere, with flowering central
boulevards and four-story apartment blocks, Bedouin encampments under
tents and wood shacks, modern high-rises, and Arab villages. At night it sets
past Tel Aviv over shimmering waters lined by modern hotels, office towers,
and places of entertainment where people, even in times of tension, are
having about as much fun as anywhere on earth.

SERVICE FOR ALL

The army: Israel's great
unifying experience.

The music you hear in your taxi is a mix of Western and Oriental sounds, and your eyes widen as the driver casually crosses the center line into oncoming traffic to go around a bus—until you are around long enough to see that they all do it, including the buses, and that it is just one more small thing that defines the Israeli experience. In many towns commerce is still small and organic, with busy main streets crammed with mom-and-pop stores and small national chains that operate without gloss; small French-built sandwich vans run deliveries all day long, along with a variety of scooters, three-wheeled bicycles, donkey-pulled carts, German trucks, and English lorries.

Depending on where you are the majority of heads you see are bare, but yarmulkes are routine in almost every community, workplace, store, restaurant, or beach. Out on the roads between towns you grow used to the sight of soldiers hitchhiking, trying to get to the base for the day or home on the weekends, and the daily appearance of young faces—men and women— lining the country's roads in an organic swirl of green khaki, which eventually becomes a reassuring pulse of continuing national vibrancy and purpose.

The national radios still wake the population each day and break most of the big news stories, continuing a tradition of service that has long passed to other media in most developed nations. Television thrives too with American dramas and comedies and local news and documentary and talk shows that help

A PART OF LIFE
The scene at an army induction center.

A NEVERENDING STRUGGLE
Soldiers on duty in Jerusalem's Old City.

A STRATEGIC PEAK

Mount Hermon, the highest point of the Golan Heights.

MISTS IN THE GALILEE

(right) The Druze village of Beit Jan, in the upper Galilee.

continue the thread of national personality and give Israel's own celebrities their place.

But you find yourself looking at celebrity differently here, for in a country packed this tight they stand in line with you at the theater or sit a few tables away at the café, and you realize that in Israel, everyone is approachable, everyone is available for conversation, and, more broadly, everyone is involved with everyone else, bound through some ineffable sense of family and interconnectedness. Everywhere people are telling other people what to do, issuing unsolicited advice and lectures, interacting in stores and on street corners as if, indeed, they were members of the same family.

Similarly the nation of six million still gossips together. Critical information about the nature of things, about what really happened in a political scandal, a business deal, a military operation is transmitted from home to home, even as the military censor muffles full disclosure of details related to national security; they flow anyway, just informally.

In the halls of a rectangular granite building on a hilltop above the Old City, Knesset members

THE HIDDEN DESERT

The vast, beautiful expanse of the
Negev Desert.

ANCIENT WAYS

(right) A traditional Bedouin home,
or *cusha*.

A SYMBOL OF PERMANENCE

(opposite) A view of the
cliff at Mount Arbel.

representing every segment of a diverging and changing society engage in
debate over crucial matters of state and an endless array of legal wrangling.
Special committees investigating some national disgrace are virtually never out
of business. Occasionally, the forces of history, politics, and honor unite and the
nation takes a cosmic leap forward, as it did with the establishment of the
national water carrier, the Eichmann trial, and the peace with Egypt.

M eanwhile, away from the glare, in small urban apartments and rural kibbutzim, in desert towns, beachfront towers, and in forgotten corners of a busy nation, a dwindling generation of founders and survivors slips away, one quiet death at a time.

The passing of the founding generation is the cardinal trait of a nation reaching its 50th anniversary. Although some of Israel's founders remain—Shimon Peres, Yitzhak Shamir, Ezer Weizman, and their contemporaries—they represent the rear guard of a generation mostly gone, a generation whose entire existence was centered around the creation of the state.

And so the second 50 years of the modern state called Israel opens with a new generation at the helm, a generation that will add its interpretations, its unique experiences, and its own sense of destiny to the national idea. Across the centuries, back to a time we know only from scriptures, this has been the most tenuous and yet the most unyielding commandment of Jewish life: to pass the national idea forward, to keep it alive, and to lead and inspire the next generation to do the same.

The founders and first citizens of modern Israel—its builders and defenders, its unknown heroes and unseen laborers—were true to this commandment. And so it remains only to see how the newest "children of Israel" adapt this ancestral gift of nationhood to the relentless challenges of life and change in a new millennium.

The torch, its flame wind-whipped but proud, has been passed. The story journeys on.

INTO THE FUTURE

The annual Independence Day air
show over the Mediterranean coast
attracts tens of thousands from Tel
Aviv to Haifa.

STORY WITHOUT END

The Old City, a new year.

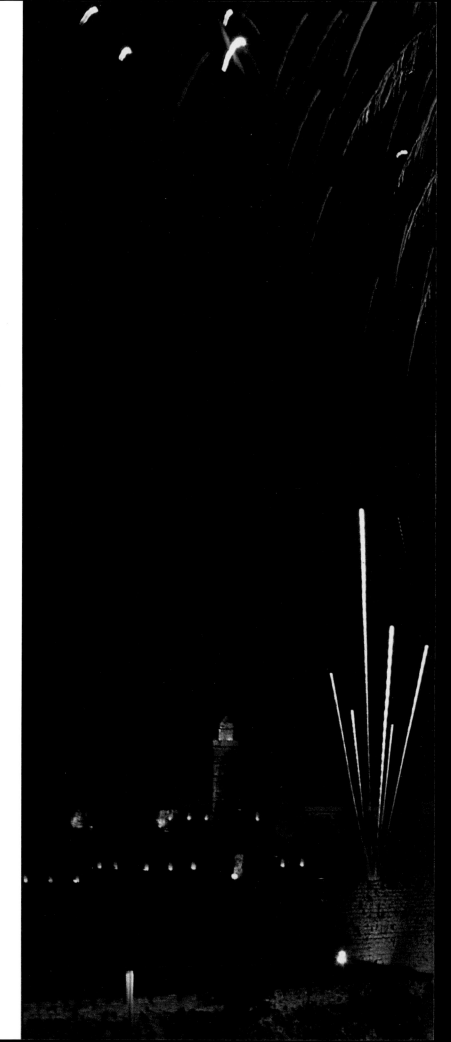

TIMELINE
OF EVENTS

< Half a Century of Independence 1948–1998 >

1948

- David Ben-Gurion declares the establishment of the State of Israel
- Israel is immediately recognized by the United States and the USSR, followed by other countries
- War of Independence begins; in 15 months of intermittent fighting, all invaders are repulsed
- Israel Defense Forces (IDF) is founded, incorporating all the pre-state defense organizations
- First census finds a population of 872,700 — 716,700 Jews and 156,000 non-Jews
- Israeli lira replaces British pound as official currency, with identical value
- Mass emigration from postwar Europe and Arab countries begins; in the years 1948–52, immigration was to bring 687,000 people to Israel's shores, doubling its Jewish population
- Count Bernadotte, U.N.-appointed mediator, is assassinated in Jerusalem
- The *Altalena*, a ship of the underground Irgun, is sunk offshore of Tel Aviv by IDF guns

1949

- First Knesset (parliament) elections; David Ben-Gurion heads a Labor-led coalition government
- First Knesset meets in Jerusalem
- Chaim Weizmann is elected Israel's first president by the Knesset
- Umm Rashrash, today Eilat, is captured by the IDF; a makeshift flag, drawn with ink, is raised
- Jerusalem is declared the capital of Israel
- Israel admitted to the United Nations as its 59th member

- The Weizmann Institute of Science is inaugurated in Rehovot
- Armistice agreements are signed with Egypt, Jordan, Syria, and Lebanon; Jerusalem is divided between Israel and Jordan, with Jordan controlling the Old City and east Jerusalem, and Israel controlling the western and southern parts of the city
- The government institutes *tzena*, rationing of food and other necessities
- First *ulpan*—special classes for intensive teaching of Hebrew—is opened
- Operation Magic Carpet—immigration of Jews from Yemen—begins
- Theodor Herzl, who died in 1904 and was buried in Vienna, is reinterred in Jerusalem
- Israel's population exceeds one million

1950

- The Knesset and most government ministries move to Jerusalem; the Knesset convenes in temporary quarters until the completion of its permanent home in 1966
- Operation Ezra and Nehemiah, bringing Jews to Israel from Iraq, begins
- First temporary camp for new immigrants is established
- The Law of Return, granting Jews the right to come as immigrants and become citizens, is passed
- The Eilat port is opened
- Great Britain recognizes Israel
- The Nazis and Nazi Collaborators (Punishment) Law is passed

1951

- A seamens strike paralyzes Israel's ports for many months
- The Hula Valley reclamation project, turning swampland into arable land, begins
- An incident in El-Hama starts a series of clashes with Syria
- Elections to the Second Knesset
- The Zionist Congress convenes in Jerusalem for the first time

1952

- Reparations agreement with Germany is signed despite protest demonstrations
- Yitzhak Ben-Zvi is elected Israel's second president, after the death in office of Chaim Weizmann
- Israel participates in the Olympic Games (in Helsinki) for the first time
- Operation Coresh—immigration of Iranian Jewry—begins

1953

- Yad Vashem (Israel's Holocaust memorial) is established in Jerusalem

- Ministry of Foreign Affairs is moved to Jerusalem
- Security situation on border with Jordan worsens; many infiltration incidents occur
- Diplomatic relations between Israel and the USSR are broken off
- Moshe Dayan is appointed chief of general staff of the IDF
- The Academy of the Hebrew Language is founded
- Prime Minister David Ben-Gurion retires to Kibbutz Sde Boker

1954

- Moshe Sharett becomes prime minister
- Egypt stops Israeli freighter *Bat Galim* from passing through the Suez Canal, in contravention of the armistice agreement
- Israeli intelligence fiasco in Egypt causes a scandal that continues for nearly a decade and forces Israel's minister of defense, Pinchas Lavon, to resign
- Amid growing anti-Semitism, emigration from North Africa accelerates
- Infiltrators from across the Jordanian border attack a bus at Ma'ale Akrabim in the northern Negev and murder 11 passengers

1955

- The four remaining Dead Sea Scrolls, acquired for the state of Israel by Professor Yigael Yadin, arrive in Israel
- A small quantity of oil is found in the Heletz oilfield in the Negev
- Elections held for the Third Knesset; David Ben-Gurion again becomes prime minister
- Bar Ilan University, with its emphasis on Jewish heritage studies, is opened in Ramat Gan
- Two Egyptian Jews are hanged after being convicted of spying for Israel
- Prime Minister of Burma U Nu pays an official visit to Israel—the first by any state leader
- Bulgarian fighter planes down an El Al civilian airliner over Bulgaria; 58 killed

1956

- Incursions of armed infiltrators across the border with Egypt increase, resulting in many casualties
- The National Religious Party is established
- Golda Meir becomes minister of foreign affairs, replacing Moshe Sharett
- Egyptian President Nasser nationalizes the Suez Canal
- France gives Israel military aid
- Following an Egyptian blockade of the Straits of Tiran, a Sinai campaign is launched by Israel, parallel to a British and French operation; in the course of

the fighting, Israel captures the Gaza Strip and the entire Sinai peninsula
- Tel Aviv University is opened
- IDF soldiers open fire on Arab villagers violating curfew in Kafr Kassem, killing 49

1957

- Israel withdraws from the Gaza Strip and the Sinai Peninsula, with assurances of free passage for its shipping through the Suez Canal
- The draining of the Hula swamp is completed, providing arable land and preventing malaria
- The Mann Auditorium is inaugurated in Tel Aviv
- Emigration from Eastern European countries increases—especially from Poland and Hungary, as well as from Egypt

1958

- MASHAV Center for International Cooperation is established by the Ministry of Foreign Affairs to share development know-how
- The first International Bible Contest is held in Jerusalem
- The cornerstone for the Knesset building is laid in Jerusalem
- Egypt and Syria unite to form the United Arab Republic
- The Supreme Court finds Israel Kastner innocent of collaboration with the Nazis
- The Hebrew University campus at Givat Ram is inaugurated
- Israel's population exceeds two million

1959

- The Employment Service is established
- Heichal Shlomo—seat of the Chief Rabbinate—is inaugurated
- Austerity rationing (*tzena*) ends
- Elections held for the Fourth Knesset
- A series of riots with an ethnic-socioeconomic basis occur in the Haifa suburb of Wadi Salib; the Navy's first submarine, the *Tanin* ("crocodile"), arrives in Haifa
- Habima is declared the national theater of Israel

1960

- Hadassah Hospital and Hebrew University Medical School are inaugurated at Ein Karem in Jerusalem
- Letters from the Bar Kochba archive (second century CE) are discovered in a dig in the Judean Desert
- The National Commission for Space Research is founded

- Operation Yachin, which brings emigrants from Morocco to Israel, commences
- The *Egoz*, carrying emigrants from Morocco, sinks; 43 passengers drown
- The Shavit II, an experimental meteorological satellite, is launched
- Adolf Eichmann, organizer of the Nazi extermination program during World War II, stands trial in Jerusalem; he is found guilty and sentenced to death for crimes against humanity and the Jewish people, and is hanged in 1962
- Israel Ber, military historian and adviser to the minister of defense, is arrested for spying for the USSR and sentenced to 15 years in prison
- Elections held for the Fifth Knesset

1962

- Yerid Hamizrach, an international commercial fair, opens in Tel Aviv; 33 countries participate
- An economic program that includes a large devaluation of the lira (Israel's currency) and the cancellation of subsidies on basic commodities leads to inflation and a rise of the deficit in the balance of trade

1963

- President Zvi Ben-Joseph dies in office; Zalman Shazar elected Israel's third president
- Levi Eshkol becomes prime minister after the resignation of David Ben-Gurion
- Haifa University is opened
- Archaeological excavations begin at Masada under the direction of Prof. Yigael Yadin

1964

- Pope Paul VI visits Israel; President Shazar receives him in Megiddo
- The Palestine Liberation Organization is founded
- The National Water Carrier, bringing water from the north and center of the country to the semi-arid south, is completed
- Ze'ev Jabotinsky, father of Revisionist Zionism, who died in 1940, is reinterred in Jerusalem
- Yitzhak Rabin is chosen as military chief of general staff
- The Nature Reserves Authority is founded

1965

- The PLO's first terrorist act, an attack on the National Water Carrier, occurs
- Eli Cohen, an Israeli agent, is hanged in Damascus
- The Israel Museum in Jerusalem is founded as the country's national museum

- Teddy Kollek becomes mayor of Jerusalem; his term of office, after being re-elected six times, lasts 28 years
- Elections held for the Sixth Knesset
- Israel and Germany establish diplomatic relations
- Neot Kedumim, a biblical landscape reserve, is founded

1966

- The permanent Knesset building is inaugurated in Jerusalem
- Hebrew writer S.Y. Agnon is corecipient of the Nobel Prize for literature
- Abie Natan, Israeli peace activist, flies to Egypt
- Despite an Arab boycott, Coca-Cola announces its plans to open a plant in Israel
- An economic plan calling for less government spending and less private consumption leads to an excessive slowdown of the economy and mass unemployment
- Educational television broadcasts begin

1967

- Israel faces massive military buildups by the neighboring Arab states and an Egyptian blockade of the Straits of Tiran. On June 5 Israel launches a preemptive strike; the West Bank, Gaza, the Sinai Peninsula, the Golan Heights, and Jerusalem come under Israeli control
- Sea-to-sea missiles fired from Egyptian missile boats near Port Said sink the Israeli destroyer *Eilat*; 47 are killed or missing and presumed dead
- U.N. General Assembly Resolution 242 adopted, providing a framework for settling the Arab-Israel dispute
- Military government is established in administered areas
- Ben-Gurion University of the Negev is opened

1968

- The submarine *Dakar* disappears on its maiden voyage in the Mediterranean
- Mapai, Ahdut Ha'avoda, and Rafi join together to form the Israel Labor Party
- Jews return to Hebron, abandoned in 1929 when more than 60 Jews there were massacred; after months they are allowed to establish a new settlement nearby, Kiryat Arba
- Israel television broadcasts begin
- The PLO formulates its covenant, which negates the existence of Israel
- Palestinian terror attacks intensify, including the hijacking of an El Al plane from Rome to Algeria

- War of attrition with Egypt and Jordan causes heavy casualties on both sides
- A car bomb in the Mahane Yehuda market in Jerusalem kills 12, injures 70

1969

- Prime Minister Levi Eshkol dies in office; Golda Meir becomes prime minister
- Five French-built torpedo boats, purchased and paid for by Israel, are successfully brought from Cherbourg port to Haifa, despite French arms embargo
- Elections held for Seventh Knesset; Meir remains prime minister
- War of attrition, sporadic military actions by Egypt along the Suez Canal, escalates until a renewed cease-fire is achieved
- Phantom planes acquired from the United States arrive in Israel

1970

- Twelve children from Moshav Avivim are killed in a terrorist attack
- Refuseniks in the USSR are sentenced to death for hijacking an airplane
- Black September: In an attempt by the PLO to take control of the country, clashes between Jordanian forces and the PLO end in Jordanian victory; the PLO regroups in Lebanon
- A series of hijackings of international airliners is perpetrated by Palestinian terrorists
- Israel's population exceeds three million

1971

- Black Panthers, a radical protest movement of Israelis of Middle Eastern and North African background, is active for some time; some of its members later enter politics
- Intensive American efforts to reach a settlement between Israel and Egypt bear no fruit
- Israel's consul general in Istanbul is killed by terrorists

1972

- The IDF frees the hostages from a hijacked Sabena plane at Lod Airport
- Three Japanese terrorists open fire at Lod airport, killing 25 and injuring 72
- Eleven Israeli athletes are murdered by PLO terrorists at the Munich Olympic Games
- Emigration from the USSR increases, totaling some 100,000 Jews in the 1970s
- The satellite communication station in Emek Ha'ela is opened
- Several letter bombs are sent to Israeli embassies abroad; Israel's agricultural attaché in London is killed

- A Libyan civilian plane is erroneously downed by the IDF in Sinai
- Ephraim Katzir becomes Israel's fourth president
- The Herut Movement and the Liberal Party join to form the Likud Party
- Israel's military attaché in Washington is killed by terrorists
- Yom Kippur War, On the Day of Atonement, the holiest day of the Jewish year, breaks out; Egypt and Syria launch a coordinated surprise attack; repulsed by Israel after fierce fighting and heavy losses, the U.N. General Assembly passes Resolution 338, calling for a settlement of the Arab-Israel conflict on the basis of Resolution 242 of 1967
- David Ben-Gurion, first prime minister, regarded as the father of the state of Israel, dies
- Elections held for the Eighth Knesset; Golda Meir reelected

- Agranat Commission appointed to investigate the causes of the unreadiness and thus the initial losses of the IDF during the Yom Kippur War; the commission concluded that the senior military officers, not the political leadership, was responsible
- Antigovernment protest demonstrations take place
- Golda Meir resigns; Yitzhak Rabin becomes prime minister
- Twenty-one youths are killed in terrorist attack in Ma'alot
- Separation-of-forces agreement signed with Egypt
- Disengagement agreement is signed with Syria
- Gush Emunim, a movement claiming Jewish rights over historical Israel (advocating settling "Judea and Samaria"—the West Bank) becomes active
- First Arthur Rubinstein Piano Competition takes place
- The U.S.-Israel Binational Science Foundation to foster civilian research is founded

- U.N. General Assembly equates Zionism with racism
- Israel signs treaty with the European Community, instituting a free trade area for industrial products and leading to a significant increase in trade
- Terrorists landing by sea attack Savoy Hotel in Tel Aviv; three IDF soldiers are killed in clash
- Suez Canal is reopened by Egypt after eight years
- Israel exhibits the Kfir, an aircraft designed and produced in Israel
- The Knesset passes law mandating direct elections of mayors and heads of local councils

1976

- In Entebbe, Uganda, the IDF frees hostages who had been captured by terrorists during the hijacking of an airliner en route to Paris; Lt. Col. Jonathan Netanyahu is killed during the action
- Prime Minister Yitzhak Rabin resigns because of domestic scandal
- Good Fence policy instituted between Israel and Lebanon
- Land Day is marked by Israeli Arabs for the first time; in protest over confiscation of Arab land, demonstrations and clashes with police leave six dead
- Yigael Yadin establishes the Democratic Movement for Change

1977

- Elections held for the Ninth Knesset; Likud party wins, ending 29 years of Labor Party rule; Menachem Begin becomes prime minister
- Egyptian President Anwar Sadat visits Jerusalem, breaking the cycle of Arab rejection of Israel
- Maccabi Tel Aviv basketball team wins European Championship
- Prime Minister Begin permits a group of Vietnamese boat refugees to enter Israel
- Project Renewal to improve the quality of life for inhabitants of distressed urban neighborhoods and towns commences

1978

- A bus is hijacked by terrorists on the coastal road; 35 passengers are killed
- Operation Litani, an action against PLO strongholds in southern Lebanon in response to attacks on civilians in northern Israel, begins
- Peace Now movement is founded
- Diaspora Museum is opened in Tel Aviv
- Yitzhak Navon becomes Israel's fifth president and first Sephardi to hold the office
- President Jimmy Carter helps negotiate Camp David accords, constituting a basis for peace between Israel and Egypt, as well for comprehensive peace in the Middle East
- Begin and Sadat awarded Nobel Peace Prize for their efforts to bring peace to the Middle East

1979

- Peace Treaty is signed with Egypt, ending a 30-year cycle of war
- El-Arish is returned to Egypt in accordance with the peace treaty
- The United Kibbutz Movement is founded

1980

- Israeli Embassy is opened in Cairo
- Basic Law: "Jerusalem, Capital of Israel" is passed by Knesset
- Inflation continues to soar; lira is replaced by shekel (1 shekel = 10 liras)
- Israel continues its withdrawal from Sinai, including the Refidim air base
- The number of tourists arriving annually exceeds one million for the first time
- Israel's exports surpass $10 billion

1981

- Maccabi Tel Aviv basketball team wins the European Championship for the second time
- Iraqi nuclear reactor is destroyed by the Israeli air force weeks before it is due to become operational
- Elections held for the Tenth Knesset; by narrowest margin, Menachem Begin reelected
- The Golan Heights Law is passed by the Knesset, effectively annexing the area

1982

- Attaché at Israel's embassy in Paris killed by terrorists
- Israel completes withdrawal from Sinai in accordance with the Israel-Egypt peace treaty, despite protest
- Israel's ambassador in London severely wounded by terrorists
- "Operation Peace for Galilee" is launched against PLO strongholds in Lebanon; within two months thousands of PLO fighters leave Beirut for Tunisia. After Israel's ally President-elect Bashir Jemayel is assassinated, Christian Phalangist forces massacre Muslim refugees at Sabra and Shatilla camps; in Israel, hundreds of thousands demonstrate against war; 75 killed in bombing of IDF headquarters in Tyre
- Sha'are Tzedek Hospital, founded in 1902, inaugurates its modern new building in Jerusalem
- Israel's population exceeds four million

1983

- Peace Now activist killed when a Jewish extremist throws a grenade
- Chaim Herzog is elected sixth president
- Menachem Begin resigns; Yitzhak Shamir succeeds him
- A major stock exchange crisis threatens the economy
- A truck loaded with explosives in Tyre kills 60 Israelis and Arabs, and wounds dozens

1984

- Terrorists take over a bus on its way from Tel Aviv to Ashkelon, killing one passenger
- Jewish underground operating in Judea and Samaria is uncovered and its members given prison sentences ranging from eight years to life; most are pardoned by the president after several years in prison
- Elections for the Eleventh Knesset result in 60–60 split; a national unity government is formed, with a rotation of prime ministers; Shimon Peres becomes prime minister
- Operation Moses brings to Israel some 7,000 Jews from the ancient Jewish community of Ethiopia

1985

- Israel Aircraft Industries unveils the first prototype of the Lavi fighter plane; the program is later discontinued for budgetary reasons
- Free trade agreement is signed with the United States
- More than 1,000 guerrillas imprisoned in Israel are exchanged for three Israeli POWs from the Lebanon war
- Israel withdraws from Lebanon, retaining a "security zone" to protect northern Israel
- An emergency stabilization program put into effect by the government succeeds in lowering annual inflation from 445 percent to 20 percent
- Administrative attaché at Israel embassy in Cairo killed by terrorists
- The new Israeli shekél replaces the shekel: NIS 1 = IS 1,000
- An Egyptian soldier opens fire on a group of Israeli tourists and kills seven
- Jonathan Pollard, convicted of spying for Israel in the United States, gets life imprisonment

1986

- Diplomatic relations established with Spain
- Anatoly (Natan) Sharansky, well-known refusenik in the USSR, arrives in Israel as a new immigrant
- Israel embassy employee in Cairo killed by terrorists
- Prime Minister Shimon Peres meets with King Hassan II in Morocco
- Ron Arad, Israeli Air Force navigator, is captured in Lebanon; his fate is still unknown
- Yitzhak Shamir returns to premiership as part of the rotation agreement signed in 1984
- An Israel interest office is opened in Warsaw, reestablishing limited diplomatic ties between Israel and a communist country

1987

- The trial of John Demjanjuk, accused of murdering Jews during World War II, opens in Jerusalem; he is found guilty but later acquitted on appeal for lack of evidence
- Intifada uprising starts in West Bank and Gaza
- The Germany-Israel Foundation for Scientific Research and Development founded; it supports basic and applied research in areas of mutual interest

1988

- Israel and the United States begin cooperation on the production of the Arrow missile
- Elections held for Twelfth Knesset; Yitzhak Shamir remains prime minister of national unity government
- An Israeli Consulate is opened in Moscow

1989

- Taba is returned to Egypt after international arbitration
- The New Israeli Opera opens its doors
- Sixteen bus passengers are killed on the Jerusalem-Tel Aviv highway as a terrorist gains control of a bus and drives it over a cliff
- A Syrian pilot defects to Israel, landing a MIG-23 at Megiddo

1990

- Mass emigration of Jews from the Soviet Union begins; within several years, almost 800,000 immigrants arrive
- The national unity government falls after a no-confidence vote; immediately thereafter, Labor Party ministers resign; a new government of right-wing and religious parties is formed
- The Israeli satellite Ofek 2 is launched into space
- Diplomatic relations with the USSR and other Eastern European countries are reestablished
- Terror attack on Israeli tourists in Egypt kills 10
- Israel's GDP growth rises to some six percent; this will continue throughout the early 1990s

1991

- Israel is attacked with Iraqi Scud missiles during Gulf War
- Operation Solomon brings most of the Jews remaining in Ethiopia, some 15,000, to Israel in a massive airlift

- Middle East Peace Conference convenes in Madrid, bringing together representatives of Israel, Egypt, Jordan, Syria, Lebanon, and the Palestinians
- U.N. General Assembly rescinds the resolution equating Zionism with racism
- Israel's population exceeds five million

1992

- Israel and China establish diplomatic relations
- Knesset passes law providing for direct election of the prime minister, to take effect from the elections for the Fourteenth Knesset (1996)
- An attack on Israel's embassy in Buenos Aires leaves 29 dead and dozens wounded
- Elections held for Thirteenth Knesset; Yitzhak Rabin of the Labor Party becomes prime minister
- Israel wins its first Olympic medals—silver and bronze in judo
- The new Supreme Court building is opened

1993

- Benjamin Netanyahu is elected chairman of the Likud Party
- Ezer Weizman is elected Israel's seventh president
- Operation "Accountability" launched after continued Katyusha attacks on northern Israel; IDF attacks Hezbollah bases in southern Lebanon
- First Israel-PLO agreement signed after secret negotiations in Oslo; PLO recognizes Israel, and Israel recognizes PLO as the representative of the Palestinian people
- Diplomatic relations are established between Israel and the Holy See

1994

- A Jewish extremist kills 29 Muslim worshippers in Hebron
- Hamas begins suicide bombing campaign in Israel; in Tel Aviv, suicide bomber blows up a bus, killing 24 and wounding dozens
- Israel and PLO sign detailed agreement on autonomy in Gaza and Jericho
- Israel-Jordan peace treaty is signed, establishing full diplomatic relations between the two states
- Morocco and Tunisia interest offices are opened
- Yitzhak Rabin, Shimon Peres, and PLO leader Yasser Arafat are awarded Nobel Peace Prize

1995

- Interim Agreement on the West Bank and the Gaza Strip is signed by Israel and the PLO, providing for broadened self-government by the Palestinians

- Prime Minister Yitzhak Rabin is assassinated by a Jewish extremist at a peace rally; Shimon Peres becomes prime minister
- Treaty of Association is signed with EU, broadening trade relations
- IDF redeploys in West Bank, turning over six main cities to the Palestinian Authority
- The number of tourists arriving annually exceeds two million for the first time

1996

- A series of suicide attacks in Jerusalem, Ashkelon, and Tel Aviv kills more than 60 Israelis
- Operation Grapes of Wrath against terrorist bases in Lebanon is launched; about 100 refugees killed in mistaken bombing of U.N. camp in Kafr Kana
- Trade representation offices are established in Oman and Qatar
- Elections held for Fourteenth Knesset and first direct elections for prime minister; Benjamin Netanyahu of the Likud is elected prime minister
- The Western Wall Tunnel is opened to the public; violent Palestinian riots follow
- Israel's per-capita GDP nears $17,000 annually, placing it 21st in the world

1997

- After months of wrangling, Netanyahu government pulls out of most of Hebron and commits to continuing peace process
- The crash of two helicopters in northern Israel kills 73 soldiers
- Seven schoolgirls are murdered by a Jordanian soldier at Naharayim, on the border between Israel and Jordan
- Suicide bombers in Jerusalem kill 21 in two separate attacks
- Industry continues to make international-level strides in medical electronics, agrotechnology, telecommunications, fine chemicals, computer hardware and software, and diamond cutting and polishing, making Israel an industry leader toward the 21st century
- Israel releases Hamas founder Ahmed Yassin after botched attempt to kill a Hamas leader in Jordan causes scandal

1998

- Israel reaches 50

Note: This material is based in part on a timeline produced by the Israeli Government Press Office

BIBLIOGRAPHY

THE JEWISH STATE (DER JUDENSTAAT), **Theodor Herzl**, Dover Publications, NYC, 1998 (originally published in Vienna, 1886).

THE HEBREW STATE, **Zeev Jabotinsky**, T. Kopp Press, Tel Aviv, 1937.

FROM HERZL TO RABIN AND BEYOND, **Amnon Rubinstein**, Schocken, Tel Aviv, 1997.

1949—THE FIRST ISRAELIS, **Tom Segev**, Domino Press, Jersusalem, 1984.

THE NEW ISRAELIS, **Yossi Melman**, Schocken, Tel Aviv, 1993.

A HISTORY OF ISRAEL—FROM THE RISE OF ZIONISM TO OUR TIME, **Howard M. Sachar**, Alfred A. Knopf, New York, 1993.

THE TRIUMPH OF EMBARRASSMENT, **Reuven Pedatzur**, Bitan, Tel Aviv, 1996.

POLITICAL DICTIONARY OF THE STATE OF ISRAEL, **Susan Hattis Rolef, Editor,** The Jerusalem Publishing House, Jerusalem, 1987, 1993.

BATTLING FOR PEACE, **Shimon Peres & David Landau, Editor,** Weidenfeld & Nicolson, London, 1995.

A PLACE AMONG THE NATIONS, **Benjamin Netanyahu**, Yediot Aharonot Publishing, Tel Aviv, 1995.

MY LIFE, **Golda Meir,** Dell Publishing, New York, 1975.

O, JERUSALEM!, **Larry Collins and Dominique LaPierre**; Simon & Schuster, New York, 1972.

INDEX

PHOTO CREDITS

Page

8: Government Press Office (GPO)
9: GPO
10: GPO
11: Itamar Grinberg
12: GPO
13: Dan Perry
14: GPO
15: Itamar Grinberg
17: Itamar Grinberg
18: Itamar Grinberg
19: Itamar Grinberg
20: Hanan Isachar
21: Hanan Isachar
22: Itamar Grinberg
23: Itamar Grinberg
26: Itamar Grinberg
27: Itamar Grinberg
28: Itamar Grinberg
29: Hanan Isachar
30: Itamar Grinberg
30a: Itamar Grinberg
31: Itamar Grinberg
32: Hanan Isachar
34: Itamar Grinberg
35: Itamar Grinberg
36: Itamar Grinberg
37: Itamar Grinberg
39: Hanan Isachar
40: Hanan Isachar
42: Itamar Grinberg
43: Hanan Isachar
45: Itamar Grinberg
46: GPO
47: GPO
48: GPO
49: GPO
50: GPO
51: GPO
52: GPO
53: GPO
54: GPO
55: GPO
56: GPO

57: GPO
58: GPO
59: GPO
61: GPO
63: GPO
64: GPO
66: GPO
67: GPO
68: GPO
70: GPO
71: GPO
72: GPO
74: GPO
75: GPO
76: GPO
77: David Eldan
78: GPO
79: GPO
80: GPO
81: GPO
82: GPO
83: GPO
84: GPO
86: David Eldan
87: GPO
88: GPO
89: GPO
90: GPO
92: GPO
95: GPO
96: GPO
98: GPO
100: GPO
101: GPO
102: GPO
104: GPO
105: GPO
107: GPO
108: GPO
109: GPO
110: GPO
113: David Rubinger
115: David Rubinger
118: David Rubinger
119: GPO

120: GPO
123: GPO
124: GPO
125: GPO
126: GPO
127: GPO
129: GPO
130: GPO
132: GPO
133: GPO
134: GPO
135: GPO
137: GPO
138: GPO
139: GPO
140: GPO
141: GPO
143: GPO
144: Yaacov Sa'ar
145: Yaacov Sa'ar
146: GPO
147: GPO
148: GPO
149: GPO
150: GPO
151: GPO
153: GPO
154: GPO
155: GPO
157: GPO
158: GPO
159: Zvika Israeli
160: The Associated Press
161: (Shamir) The Associated Press
161: (Hebron) GPO
162: GPO
163: GPO
165: GPO
166: GPO
167: GPO
168: GPO
169: GPO
170: GPO
171: GPO

172: GPO
173: GPO
174: GPO
176: Ya'acov Sa'ar
177: Ya'acov Sa'ar
178: GPO
179: Avi Ohayon
180: GPO
181: GPO
182: GPO
184: GPO
185: GPO
187: GPO
189: GPO
190: (Layers) Itamar Grinberg
190: (Hebron) GPO
191: Itamar Grinberg
192: Itamar Grinberg
194: Itamar Grinberg
197: Hanan Isachar
198: Itamar Grinberg
199: Itamar Grinberg
200: Itamar Grinberg
201: Hanan Isachar
204: Hanan Isachar
205: Itamar Grinberg
206: Itamar Grinberg
207: Tal Schpanzer
208: Hanan Isachar
209: Hanan Isachar
210: Tal Schpanzer
211: Dan Perry
212: Itamar Grinberg
213: IDF Archives (top) Nir Kafri (bottom)
214: Itamar Grinberg
215: Itamar Grinberg
216: Itamar Grinberg
217: Hanan Isachar
219: Itamar Grinberg
220: Itamar Grinberg
221: Hanan Isachar